# THE HEAVENLY LADDER

# THE
# HEAVENLY
# LADDER

## The Jewish Guide
## to Inner Growth

*Edward Hoffman*

Illustrations by Harvey Gitlin

*1817*

Harper & Row, Publishers, San Francisco

Cambridge, Hagerstown, New York, Philadelphia
London, Mexico City, São Paulo, Singapore, Sydney

FIRST EDITION

Library of Congress Cataloging-in-Publication Data

Hoffman, Edward.
  The heavenly ladder.

  Bibliography: p.
  Includes index.
  1. Spiritual life—Judaism.   2. Jewish way of life.
I. Title.
BM723.H64   1985        296.7′4        85-42779
ISBN 0-06-064001-4

85  86  87  88  89  MPC  10  9  8  7  6  5  4  3  2  1

To my son, Jeremy Isaac,
who climbs the Ladder with joy

# CONTENTS

# ACKNOWLEDGMENTS

This book would not have been possible without the valuable cooperation of many people. Professors Gerald Epstein of the Mount Sinai Medical School, W. Edward Mann of York University, and Howard Schwartz of the University of Missouri, St. Louis, provided much encouragement as well as conceptual contributions. For their valued enthusiasm, gratitude is similarly extended to Harvey Gitlin, Aaron Hostyk, Rabbi Neal Kaunfer, Arthur Kurzweil, and Paul Palnik. I wish to convey special thanks for their unflagging emotional support throughout the progress of the writing to my parents and my brother; to Gertrude Brainin and Dorothy Smith; and, above all, to my wife, Laurel. The editorial excitement and judgment of Sharon LeBell and John Loudon are also considerably appreciated.

Jacob left Beer-sheba, and went toward Haran. And he came to a certain place, and stayed there that night, because the sun had set. Taking one of the stones of the place, he put it under his head and lay down in that place to sleep. And he dreamed that there was a ladder set up on the earth, and the top of it reached to heaven; and behold, the angels of God were ascending and descending on it!

GENESIS 28:10–12

# PREFACE

Since my childhood days in *yeshiva*, (Hebrew day school),*
I have been impressed by the practical insights into daily life shown
by the great Jewish sages. Even at that tender age I marveled at the
wisdom with which the rabbis of old could swiftly resolve questions
posed to them by men and women faced with dilemmas. At home,
my grandfather, a leading cantor in the United States, helped to
bring these ancient heroes to life. Through our frequent discussions,
I began to sense their style of reasoning, their values, and their
approach to human existence.

Later, in my training as a psychologist, I avidly absorbed the
various schools of thought that comprise the modern discipline. Yet,
as much as I prized the discoveries of Sigmund Freud and other
major thinkers, I felt decisively that something was lacking from all
such orientations. The inner world they described seemed strangely
muted, without any of the splendor I had encountered in my Jewish
studies. To me, none of the dominant scientific models of the mind
appeared to be either conceptually complete or emotionally satisfying.

Propelled by my own intuitions, however, I soon became aware
that some of the most innovative, seminal figures in psychology had
expressed great interest in the sacred aspects of human experience.
Whatever their particular vantage point, they insisted that we all
have legitimate yearnings to connect to that higher Source within.
In short, I found that I was in good company. Spurred by this
realization, I began to explore the psychological terrain of the
Jewish visionary tradition. I wrote *The Way of Splendor* and *Sparks
of Light* to chronicle my efforts in this domain.

---

* See the Glossary on page 129 for definitions of Hebrew terms.

I have become increasingly involved in a personal way with the exciting movement of Jewish spiritual renewal that is now taking place around the globe. Like others, I have discovered a growing number of Jews, from all walks of life, who are enthusiastically seeking out new and revitalized forms of liturgy and study, worship and communal intimacy. As a result of many stimulating conversations with such individuals, young and old, I have felt the need for a book that speaks ''Jewishly'' to the concerns among many for greater inner direction and wholeness.

For example, I am often asked, ''Well and good, our tradition teaches us that we each have a specific purpose here on earth. How can I find out what mine is?'' Or, ''How can I gain a better sense of direction in life? Sometimes I feel like I'm drifting from experience to experience without any goals in mind.'' Or, ''I hear there is such a thing as 'Jewish meditation.' Can it really help me to relax, to calm myself, to focus on what I need to accomplish? How can I learn more about it?''

I suspect that such questions, whether voiced aloud or silently, are felt by many thoughtful people today, eager for more satisfying inner fare. For, as the Psalms tell us, spiritual hungers are quite real.

The purpose of this book, therefore, is to provide a guide and a framework for development within, from the uplifting perspective of the Jewish sages. The focus is not only on the rationalist and ethical wisdom of Judaism, but also on its visionary, mystical aspects; both speak most relevantly to our present situation.

Reflecting my own field of training, the emphasis of this book is on Jewish experiential methods to enhance our sense of personal identity and purpose. To this end, many life-review and meditative exercises are introduced and discussed. However, in no way is this format intended to minimize the value of formal Jewish study and learning; indeed, we must awaken both facets of our being for true harmony within.

I hasten to stress that this work is not designed to reduce the spiritual vistas of Judaism to the purview of modern psychology. Rather, as our sages have always emphasized, the strengthening of our character and emotional well-being is a vital attribute of meeting the divine in our lives.

If this book manages in some small way to help you along that path, it will have fulfilled its purpose.

# INTRODUCTION

Today a growing number of Jews are experiencing an exciting spiritual renewal. This inner return, like its transcendent Source, knows no bounds of age, social background, or geographic location. Across the United States and elsewhere, those who previously felt only a weak or tenuous link to their Jewish heritage are now experiencing an increasing attraction for the sacred wisdom of their forebears.

While there are undoubtedly many causes for this worldwide phenomenon of renewal, one seems especially strong: our widespread need for a sense of roots and personal identity in these rapidly changing times. Amidst the sea of conflicting values and shifting social fads that marks our contemporary landscape, it is certainly not always easy to achieve a strong awareness of self and purpose in life. True inner growth is never simple; but in our hurried, workaday world, it is particularly difficult to know and trust our deeper impulses. When so many obviously superficial ''experts'' abound, we may sometimes forget that sages have indeed existed—and that our Jewish tradition has for millenia offered powerful means to develop our inner potential.

To be sure, our lives today are in some ways quite different from those of our predecessors. We virtually take for granted an array of political, civil, and religious rights scarcely imaginable to those who suffered under murderous persecution and oppression. To our Jewish ancestors who struggled to eke out a living amidst a hostile Gentile world, our material affluence would truly seem a dazzling gift from above.

Yet, in other respects, the basic aspects that we associate with the human condition—health, family relations, livelihood—have remained relatively constant throughout the centuries. Even a casual perusal of the writings of the sages shows that then, as now, people worried over these same issues and sought comforting advice. Indeed, more than two thousand years ago, Hillel the Elder pronounced three key questions to guide the inner direction of each person: "If I am not for myself, who will be? If I am only for myself, what am I? If not now, when?"

Have any of these concerns become obsolete in the slightest?

Many people currently suffer from recurrent bouts of depression. They feel a loss of meaning in their lives and an inability to experience daily pleasures. They move through their days as though surrounded by a wall or a dark cloud. Such mental disharmony is not simply an invention of our fast-paced, technological society. In the quiet *shtetls* or villages of Eastern Europe in the 1700s and early 1800s, Hasidic leaders were quite familiar with this troubling disorder. In their writings and public speeches—formal philosophical tracts as well as poetic folk stories—they offered their many followers specific advice on how to achieve joy and transcendence. From meditation to dance, their methods remain vibrant today.

We sometimes tend to think that ours is the only age in which men and women have found it difficult to relax or overcome inner tensions. But, for hundreds of years, Jewish sages have provided insights into the means to handle day-to-day conflicts and to acquire the true strength required to manage life's vicissitudes. In fact, Rabbi Akiba and his rabbinical colleagues grappled wiith such questions as they planned the basis for post-biblical Judaism in the second century C.E.

The Talmud relates that one day they earnestly exchanged opinions as to the single most essential personality attribute for leading a productive, worthwhile life. "With what does one lead the right way?" they asked one another. "With a good heart," Rabbi Eliezer concluded, "for all else comes from it."

Another source of Jewish knowledge about our universe within has derived from its mystical side. Thanks in part to the impeccable scholarship of Gershom Scholem and his students in Israel, it is now clear that many of the most celebrated Jewish thinkers have delved deeply into the Kabbalah—the esoteric, often hidden realm of Judaism. Inside this proverbial orchard of exotic flowerings can be found exciting ideas and methods to awaken our creative potentials.

Kabbalists have long been interested in dreams, meditation, the power of will and intentionality, the use of imagination and intuition, and other topics of considerable interest to us today. Their emphasis on the liberation of our dormant capabilities has a great deal to offer us in a practical way.

For another key reason, the Jewish tradition has a powerful message to guide our present inner development. We live in a time of perhaps unprecedented gloom and cynicism about our inborn nature. Almost since its inception, modern psychology has painted a dark, even dismal picture of our desires and impulses; outside of the bold vision of a handful of iconoclasts, we are seen to possess little more than animal-like drives for sensual gratification and related motives for selfish aggrandizement over others. Our personal willpower is viewed as a puny, helpless thing in comparison to the overruling influences from our early childhood. To many of us, such a portrait seems obviously incomplete, devoid of our most intimate longings for joy, beauty, awe, wonder, compassion, love, and transcendence.

The sages and teachers of Judaism, however, have given us a far more comprehensive vista of our innate potential. Again and again, they have affirmed that within each of us are many levels of being, and that our possibilities for accomplishment are almost endless. To this end I have incorporated many exercises, based upon age-old precepts, designed to stimulate this awareness on the reader's part.

The format of this book is as follows. The first section, "Rediscovering the Tradition," provides a historical overview to Judaism's concern for self-improvement. Chapter 1 encompasses a wide range of historical figures and movements, beginning with the early sages who lived during the destruction of the Second Temple of Jerusalem. The most recent figure examined is Rabbi Israel Salanter, founder of the important *musar* (ethics) movement in mid-nineteenth-century Lithuania. The role of Jewish legends as well as rationalist philosophy is likewise explored, together with mystical and Hasidic contributions.

The second section, "The Universe Within," sets forth some of the basic principles of self-growth, from the inspiring perspective of the major Jewish thinkers. Chapter 3 offers their central metaphysical and psychological concepts rgarding our "mission on earth." Chapter 4 forcuses on their special view of inward ascent; Jacob's vision of the heavenly ladder has long been their key symbol for this divine journey. This chapter also highlights some of their specific methods for enhancing the exciting process of emotional and spiritual development.

The third section, "Spiritual Exercises," provides definite techniques—based on traditional Jewish ideas and practice—for strengthening our higher faculties and sense of purpose in life. Nearly thirty different exercises are presented. Chapter 5 offers a variety of life-review exercises, to help you gain a deeper understanding of "from where you have come." The helpful role of others in uplifting your own outlook is pinpointed. The more accurate the map to your own mental territory, the more clear—and joyful—lies your path ahead. Chapter 6 focuses on ways to fortify your powers of will, concentration, and imagination—powerful tools that the sages have for centuries recommended to guide our strivings in life. Chapter 7 examines how the sacred letters of the Hebrew alphabet can serve to awaken our higher capabilities; indeed, this method has been a time-honored means in Judaism to help lead us to our creative Source.

From this inner realm, I am convinced, the solutions to all of our daily problems can be found.

As the Hasidic master Rabbi Nachman of Bratslav aptly taught, "Every person is a miniature world." Be patient in your explorations, and the sacred kingdom will reveal to you its hidden treasures.

## The Treasure

A man once dreamed that there was a great treasure hidden under a bridge in Vienna. As he lived in a remote village, the dream seemed absurd to him and he tried to ignore it. But night after night he experienced the same dream. Finally, he made the long journey to Vienna. There he found the bridge he had dreamed about. He dared not search for the treasure by day, because of the many people who were there. A sentry stood close by.

After several days of observing the man stand and regard the bridge, the sentry asked him, ''What are you doing here?'' The man decided that it would be best to tell the whole story and ask for help, hoping that the sentry would share the treasure with him. So he told the entire story.

The sentry replied, ''A Jew is concerned only with dreams! I also had a dream, and I also saw a treasure. It was in a small house in a village and hidden under a cellar. But who bothers with dreams?''

In relating his dream, the sentry had accurately described the man's village and house. He rushed home, dug under his cellar, and found the treasure. He said, ''Now I know that I had the treasure all along. But in order to find it, I had to travel to Vienna.''

—RABBI NACHMAN OF BRATSLAV

# 1.

# Rediscovering the Tradition

## 1

# JUDAISM AND SELF-TRANSFORMATION

In its nearly four thousand years of history Judaism has, like a dazzling crystal, shown the world many brilliant aspects. In modern times age-old Jewish notions promoting social justice and compassion for others, the rule of law and individual liberty, have been quite influential in the West. For millennia, though, Jewish sages have also addressed extensively an equally important realm: that of character development and emotional well-being. Today, when so many men and women are searching for inner stability and harmony, Judaism is extremely relevant; its inspiring ideas and methods for growth within speak to us in a most timely manner.

Historically, the major Jewish thinkers have always emphasized our capacity to lead productive, balanced, and joyful lives. They have insisted that we each are born with free will and the capability to greatly perfect ourselves and the world around us. In fact, some of Judaism's most celebrated sages have declared that every person, through diligence and sustained effort, can attain the heights of mental and spiritual achievement. We are limited, they have observed, by the barriers we impose on ourselves—barriers to the complete fulfillment of our latent potential. In the time-honored Jewish metaphor, even the loftiest gates of the divine lie open before us—if we are willing to climb the celestial ladder within.

Before we can explore Judaism's provocative teachings about our inner life, it will be helpful first to survey across the centuries some of its varied terrain of ideas. In that way, we will have a valuable context for examining in greater detail this fascinating field. We must remember that Judaism has never existed in a historical vacuum. Indeed, the sages have remarked that this sacred tradition relates to every person in every generation. Thus they have never ceased to combine the timeless with the temporal, the transcendent with the everyday.

Of course, it is impossible to discuss even in passing all the significant elements of Jewish intellectual and moral thought that bear upon our subject; such a monumental task would certainly lie outside the scope of the present volume. For this reason, the sections that follow in this chapter highlight those areas that seem most germane to our particular focus.

Our survey begins largely with the post-biblical and post-Temple era for two chief reasons: First, because over the years many observers, Jews and non-Jews alike, have sought to elucidate the practical wisdom contained within the Bible, and second, because scholars still know comparatively little about the daily lives of Jews in that ancient epoch. Undoubtedly, continuing archaeological research will reveal much exciting material for our future discovery. With this awareness in mind, let us begin our journey in the Land of Israel, more than two thousand years ago.

### The Sages and Inner Growth

From its far-distant origins in the time of Abraham, Judaism has manifested a true concern for personal behavior. On their simplest level, the biblical narratives clearly reflect an interest in elevating our inborn nature; the words and deeds of such figures as Abraham and Sarah, Moses and Aaron, are recounted anew each year, partly to provide concrete models for us to emulate. In other instances, family conflicts like those of Jacob and Esau, or Joseph and his brothers, serve to illumine our own struggles to achieve peace with others. In their thunderous exhortations for change and their stirring visions of redemption, the Prophets communicate a heavenly insistence that we choose the right way to live. But, for many hundreds of years, the dominant expression of Jewish spirituality was centered on the sacrificial observances associated with the holy Temple of Jerusalem.

After all, the most exalted moment for the entire Jewish people in that era was the entry of the High Priest into the Holy of Holies on Yom Kippur. That was the supreme moment of renewal for all. For Judaism to exist without the Temple—its divinely commanded rituals and attendant hierarchy of priests—seemed unthinkable.

Nevertheless, another increasingly important spiritual force began to rise in strength over the centuries: those individuals who interpreted biblical law and taught its day-to-day meaning to the common folk. Historians trace the beginnings of this group of teachers or sages back to Ezra the Scribe, in the fifth century B.C.E., who restored Scripture to sacred status and prescribed Jewish practice to the returning Babylonian exiles and the remnants of the indigenous population. Ezra, a priest and a scribe, is the first sage to be identified by name. He was, therefore, the precursor of the anonymous scribes (*sofrim*), who appeared in the period of Jewish history known as that of the Great Assembly. In this era, about which only meager information is available, the scribes devoted themselves to the explication of Judaism beyond its specific biblical tenets.

For a long time the priestly class and the sages maintained cordial relations and a sense of joint purpose: to serve the Almighty in holiness. Each group had its well-recognized and special role to play in sustaining the day-to-day life of the Jews. But as Persian gave way to Hellenistic dominion over Judea, conflicts between these two clusters of leadership became more and more pronounced. Following the Maccabean triumph over Macedonian forces in the second century B.C.E.—the basis for the festival of Hannukah—the Jewish priestly family of the Hasmoneans assumed direction of the nation. For economic and other reasons, the Hasmoneans, who awarded themselves the title of monarch, sought to minimize the influence of the sages or Pharisees (which, in their foes' appellation, meant "separatists"). Simultaneously, the Hasmoneans began to concentrate complete religious and political power in the hands of a wealthy elite of fellow priestly families, known as Sadducees (which meant "pious" in their self-styled naming).

Over the ensuing decades, the sages persisted in challenging the rulings of the priestly class, but usually to little avail at the time. In matters of Jewish law, practice, and belief, the Sadducees were increasingly remote from the concerns of ordinary people—farmers, laborers, artisans, and the like. Many Sadducees openly sought to emulate the Macedonian aristocracy and its Hellenistic culture in every possible way. In contrast, the sages typically spoke for the masses; most were from humble backgrounds themselves. To them, questions of daily conduct and personal development were of vital importance. As a result, the people regarded them as their true guides for both morality and visionary inspiration.

By the time Roman hegemony replaced Hellenistic dominance in the region, the great scholars had become the spiritual leaders of the Jews, even though political authority and the high priesthood were held by others. To this day individuals still ponder the many pronouncements of Hillel and Shammai—the two illustrious sages at the time of Herod's rule over Jerusalem—while even the name of the High Priest is forgotten.

Yet, despite growing resistance to the mediocrity of Sadducee leadership, the priestly class refused to relinquish its tight grip upon the temporal reigns of Judaism. Ironically, it was the disastrous revolt against Rome—and with it, the terrible destruction of the holy Temple—that finally elevated the sages and their lofty teachings to the forefront of Judaism. Such, of course, has been their position ever since.

The insurrection led by the Zealots, or political extremists, was initially successful, but it inevitably culminated in the bloody defeat of the Judean state. Following a series of astonishing victories in the years 66 and 67 C.E., the Judean forces gradually found themselves no match for the Roman legions. After regaining most of the countryside, the Romans encircled Jerusalem and prepared to beseige it. The total collapse of organized Judaism seemed imminent. Rabbi Yohanan ben Zakkai, an influential disciple of Hillel and a prominent teacher of mysticism and ethics, felt compelled to act.

According to legend, Rabbi Yohanan feigned death and escaped from Jerusalem to seek out the Roman commander Vespasian. In exchange for his allegiance, Rabbi Yohanan asked a modest request: that Vespasian spare the coastal city of Yavneh, long famous for its scholars, and permit him to establish an academy there after the war. As the sage was neither of priestly nor Davidic descent, and therefore not a political threat, Vespasian agreed.

In August of the year 70 C.E., the Romans seized and destroyed the holy Temple. Three years later they captured Masada, the last surviving Judean fortress, and the rebellion was over. These calamitious events marked the abrupt end of the sacrificial system and priestly structure of Judaism; tremendous political and social devastation simultaneously occurred. The Sanhedrin, the Jewish Supreme Court, ceased to exist. The aristocratic dominion of the priestly families and the dominance of the Sadducees in national affairs also came to a sudden close. The Zealots, who had brought on the war, were ruined. The Pietists were overcome by excessive mourning. Consequently, the Pharisees were the only cohesive group left to preserve Judaism.

Soon after the fall of Jerusalem, Rabbi Yohanan established a new Sanhedrin at Yavneh. It met in the upper story of a house and in a vineyard near a pigeon house. Upon Rabbi Yohanan's death, leadership of the sages' conclave passed to Rabbi Gamaliel II, a forceful and energetic organizer; and the Judean people soon came to regard Yavneh as the spiritual equal of Jerusalem. Between 70 and 132 C.E., it truly accomplished a great deal. There, each year, the Hebrew calendar was intercalated and the *shofar* blown. In the year 90 C.E., the Bible was canonized in one of the most significant and far-reaching acts associated with "Yavneh, the great city of scholars and rabbis."

Beginning in this period and culminating in the decades after the final Jewish revolt against Rome (132–135 C.E.), Judaism underwent an extremely powerful and enduring change of emphasis. In contemporary language, we might almost say that a paradigm shift took place in those years. Initially, many expected and then hoped that the Temple would be rebuilt in their lifetime. Leading scholars, unfamiliar with the intricacies of political wheeling and dealing, periodically led delegations to high Roman officials; but they met continual disappointment. These sages advised future generations: "Be on guard in your relations with the ruling power, for they bring no man near to them except for their own interests; seeming to be friends such time as it is to their own advantage, they stand not with a man in the hour of his need."

Apocalyptic teachings about an approaching Judgment Day also aroused much excitement at first. Even the great Rabbi Akiba, the dean of his contemporaries, was apparently caught up in such alluring speculation. He initially proclaimed the Judean solder Bar-Koziba the harbinger of the Messiah (renaming him Bar-Kochba, or Son of the Star), when he won a few early victories against Rome.

However, the brutality and horror that accompanied the Roman suppression of Bar-Kochba's rebellion decisively convinced the Jewish people that no quick reversal of their political situation lay at hand. Indeed, they could scarcely afford another apocalyptic bid for national independence. As punishment for the revolt, the Romans forbade Torah teaching, Sabbath observance, and circumcision as capital offenses. Thousands were sold into slavery. Jerusalem was rebuilt as Aelia Capitolina and no Jew was allowed within its gates. The Emperor renamed the country Palestine (Land of the Philistines), a label deliberately chosen to indicate that the territory was no longer considered Judean. Soon after the rebellion was put down, Rabbi Akiba and other leading scholars were executed for violating the ban on Torah teaching; Simon bar Yochai—Rabbi Akiba's leading disciple—and his son are said to have gone into hiding for thirteen years. In 139 C.E., Antoninus Pius initiated an easing of conditions, but the *galut* (''exile'') for the nation was indisputable.

The Torah academies now deliberately put apocalypse aside; in order for Judaism to survive, its spiritual leaders stressed, it was necessary to accept the nation's fate and strive for individual closeness to the divine. The Temple had been the *bet-ha-Mikdash*, the Holy House. But now the synagogue was a *mikdash meat*, a miniature holy place. With the Temple in ruins and Jerusalem a forbidden city, each Jew would become a High Priest, seeking heavenly favor for the nation and for himself. The nation could not free itself from the exile, but the possibility of self-renewal, *teshuvah*, lay open for all. In fact, on fast days, an elder arose in each synagogue to remind those assembled that fasting was merely a method to help them achieve greater purity in their daily lives. *Teshuvah* became the key concept—not simply repentance for one's misdeeds, but a return to the Holy Source within each person. According to the sages of the time, *teshuvah* was created even before the universe; in a way, it was seen to transcend both time and space as a supernal force in the cosmos.

During this era, the significance of Torah study also came to occupy a central position in Judaism. Study of the Torah—that is, the Bible and the oral tradition based upon it—became regarded as vital to the heavenly plan. Through sacred study, the sages declared, the divine order becomes clear and explicit. Torah study also became respected as a mystical activity, permitting the individual to draw nearer to the deity. Thus, inevitably, the scholars came to be viewed as holy figures, capable of working wonders. Some were extolled as seers and masters of arcane knowledge; but nearly all were venerated as teachers to guide men and women through the straits of day-to-day life. Indeed, the Hebrew appellation *rabbi*, which originated in this period, literally means "my teacher."

Instead of forming a separate professional class, however, the rabbis were bound up with the world of the common people. These *tannaim*, teachers, were not philosopher-kings, but working folk themselves, involved with the vicissitudes of everyday existence. More than one hundred celebrated scholars of this period were artisans, a considerable number were tradesmen, and others were physicians or practiced various professions. Some of the most renowned rabbis made their living with their hands—as carpenters, smiths, or shoemakers. None of these early sages earned their livelihood as scholars; to accept money for fulfilling the divine command was deemed a prostitution of their sacred calling.

As a result of this situation, Jewish emphasis on the practical aspects of personal growth and daily spirituality became paramount. Apocalyptic and eschatalogical speculation receded to the background of Judaism; for the rabbis were far more concerned with the patient, step-by-step path of inner ascent. Clearly reflecting this outlook, the Mishnah, the foundation of Jewish law, was completed and put into writing in the early third century C.E.

Perhaps above all other considerations, the Mishnah stressed individual self-mastery as the basis for transcendent experience. Particularly in the section *Pirkey Avoth* ("Ethics of the Fathers"), the Mishnah devoted considerable attention to both the principles and methods for attaining inner strength and identity. This tractate has traditionally held such an elevated status that it has been incorporated into the synagogue liturgy and read on Sabbath afternoons during the summer months. The Sephardim (Middle-Eastern Jews) have not followed this custom, though in Spain *Pirkey Avoth* used to be read on Sabbath mornings. Among European Jewry, the general practice has been to read its chapters on all the Sabbaths between Passover and Rosh Hashanah.

For millennia, the greatest Jewish thinkers—including the mystics—have recommended *Pirkey Avoth* as the starting place in Judaism for complete self-transformation. Such incisive spiritual teachers as Maimonides, the brilliant medieval physician and philosopher, have even considered this tractate as the basis for attaining the prophetic state. "It is clear," he wrote, "that following the discipline described in this text leads to prophecy." In the next chapter, we will examine *Pirkey Avoth*'s compelling notions in some detail.

Paralleling their emphasis on spiritual growth as a lifelong process, the sages increasingly strove to promote education for the young. Judah II, who led Jewish affairs in Palestine from c. 225 to c. 255 C.E., sought to perfect elementary Jewish education by organizing schools in every town and village. He expounded that the entire world is sustained by the breath of school children, and forbade their instruction to be interrupted, even in the awesome event of the rebuilding of the Temple in Jerusalem. But by the year 280 or so, the leading Torah academies lay in Babylonia; they were no longer in the Holy Land, where the Jewish population had lost much of its spiritual vitality.

Long after the Mishnah emerged as the definitive post-biblical text of Jewish law and belief, new generations of scholars (known as *amoraim*, interpreters) continued their discussions in both Palestine and Babylonia. These discourses comprised not only legal give-and-take on the proper way to observe Scripture (*halakha*, literally "the way to walk"), but also included non-legal material *aggadah*, tellings) involving homilies, folklore, myth, legend, and even humor. Initially, there was no clear demarcation between these two fields, and scholars were typically proficient in all branches of Jewish learning. But mastery of the growing body of *aggadah* began to require specialized training, and by the late third and early fourth centuries, the golden age of this provocative tradition took place. Eventually, necessity forced the written compilation of both *halakhic* and *aggadic* aspects of Judaism.

Within the Babylonian world, severe Byzantine suppression led to a series of Jewish rebellions. The Eastern emperors shut down the Torah academies around the year 300 C.E. Though the rulers allowed these to reopen under tight controls a few years later, the sages saw clearly that the reprieve would be only temporary. The dominant Christian society was eager to eliminate the remaining validating structures of autonomous Jewish life. Thus the Palestinian Talmud ("completion" in Hebrew) was hastily accumulated and edited, just before the Emperor Theodosius II permanently abolished Jewish self-government in Palestine.

In Babylonia, the situation was much the same; the Gemara (the commentary surrounding the Mishnah) was likewise closed due to bitter necessity. Massive persecutions and murders by the Babylonian royalty caused many Jews to fear that the centuries-old Oral Tradition would be extinguished unless it was written down. In approximately 470, half the Jews in the city of Ispahan were put to death and leading scholars executed. The survivors recognized that the time had arrived to record the oral tradition as completely as possible.

For several generations afterward, during the late fifth and sixth centuries, the *savoraim* (expositors) continued to edit the Babylonian Gemara. Far more comprehensive and thoroughly edited than its Palestinian counterpart, it quickly became accepted among world Jewry as the most important and authoritative of the two works. Significantly, Judaism has never proclaimed a precise date when the task of the *savoraim* was officially concluded.

Reflecting its process of development as scholars' notes, the Talmud is hardly a unitary work. Rather, it is an edited anthology of the deliberations of the academies where Judaism was explicated; the Talmud records views that indicate a consensus among the rabbis on a particular subject of discussion. It also reports the opinions of individual teachers. Much of the Talmud involves the intricacies of Scripture-derived law on virtually every aspect of human life—from prayer to sexual intercourse.

Yet, the Talmud also contains a tremendous amount of non-legal material, encompassing the *aggadic* realm we have previously mentioned. This material includes aphorisms about human character types, anecdotes and tales concerning biblical and post-biblical heroes, astronomical and botanical observations, medical and psychological advice, and many additional topics. There are a variety of intriguing remarks related to dreams and the mind, emotions and physical health, the nature of transcendent experience, and other topics relevant to us today.

Some of the *aggadah* is concerned with mystical notions regarding humanity and the universe. Long overlooked by modernists, these fascinating ideas are characteristically expressed in a veiled or story-like manner. In *The Essential Talmud*, Rabbi Adin Steinsaltz, the contemporary Talmudic scholar, has observed, "A considerable amount of *aggadic* material can only be understood metaphorically . . . either because the sages were reluctant to enter esoteric spheres or because they did not want to impart knowledge that might prove harmful to the unlearned listener."*

It is important to realize that the Talmud presents neither *halakha* or *aggadah* in any sort of systematic manner. The psychological references are quite scattered; indeed, much of the two-and-a-half million words of the Babylonian edition are not even written in grammatically complete sentences. The organization of the text was chiefly geared to the original necessity for memorization, as indicated by the terse style and numerous mnemonics.

Interestingly, though the Babylonian Talmud was largely closed by the sixth century, the myth-making and imaginative activity of the sages went on for nearly a thousand years. This is the intriguing realm of Judaism known as the midrash (*drash* means "searching inquiry" in Hebrew). Its ancient beginnings lie in Jewish legends that circulated in the eras of the First and Second Temple of Jerusalem. Some of this material found its way into the *aggadah*; but much remained oral in nature, taught and embellished by generations of succeeding sages and story-tellers. In particular, the rabbis liked to draw upon this imaginative, lively sphere for their synagogue sermons.

Eventually, compilations called "Midrash books" arose, with their focus the weekly Sabbath or special, holy day readings. In addition to producing these collections, anonymous editors also began to organize the material in the form of verse-by-verse commentaries on books of the Bible. Presumably, such work started in the fifth century.

The first complete Midrashic commentary of this type to be assembled was the *Midrash Rabbah on Genesis*. Genesis was in many ways the most popular book of the Bible, and lent itself especially well to various forms of *aggadic* expression. The next verse-by-verse commentary produced in this manner is believed to be the *Midrash Rabbah on Lamentations*; like its predecessor, it was probably compiled in the sixth century. Until well into the twelfth or even thirteenth centuries in Babylonia and elsewhere, additional collections of *Midrash* were set into writing and promulgated.

In modern times, this longstanding tradition fell into disrepute

---

*Please refer to the Bibliography on page 132 for complete publishing information.

and then obscurity, due to the disdain of rationalist scholars. But today it is undergoing a true renaissance of interest, as a growing number of religious writers, poets, and lay people in general have begun to recognize the beauty and vitality of Judaism's legendary and mythic aspects—and their importance for Jewish survival historically.

Aside from the poetic splendor of the Midrash, it has incorporated considerable wisdom about the human condition, as well as much hidden, esoteric knowledge. Its evocative tales—of exiled kings and disguised prophets, lost princesses and courageous heroes, friendly animals and powerful angels, secret caves and jeweled mountains—symbolically depict the landscape of our vast, inner world.

The Midrash is also filled with reverential images celebrating the divine wonders that surround us in the everyday, natural environment. This warm feeling for nature and the elements—earth, wind, fire, and water, and all growing things—undoubtedly represents an implicit balance with respect to the more patriarchal modes of *halakhic* discourse. "Just as man is endowed with a living soul," observed Angelo S. Rappoport (*Myth and Legend of Ancient Israel*) in describing the Midrashic outlook, "so the whole universe is singing the praises of and is rendering homage to the Living Creator. The sun, the moon and the stars, in a word, the entire cosmos is a living being endowed with a soul."

## Medieval Rationalism: Moses Maimonides: Philosopher-Healer

During the Middle Ages, Jewish thinkers continued to devote considerable attention to the subject of personal development. However, their emphasis tended to be more rationalist in orientation than that of their Talmudic predecessors. Indeed, some of the leading sages in this era were physicians and astronomers. They viewed the cosmos and the human individual as reflections of the divine order; the way to holiness was seen to lie in our capacity to lead healthful, purposeful lives in accordance with the sacred—and ultimately logical—principles revealed in the Torah. Many regarded such precepts as embodying rational deductions concerning the world. Especially in the Moorish civilization that long flourished in North

Africa and the Iberian peninsula, Jewish philosophers espoused this notion.

Undoubtedly, the most influential and celebrated of all such medieval figures was Maimonides (Moses ben Maimon). Over the course of his colorful lifetime, Maimonides (1135–1204) became renowned throughout the world as a scholar, philosopher, and communal leader to his fellow Jews. At the same time, he achieved international acclaim as physician to the royal family in Cairo and author of key medical works. Centuries before contemporary interest in holistic health care, Maimonides articulated ideas and prescribed practices that remain relevant to this day. Eight hundred and fifty years after his birth, he is becoming the focus of much renewed interest.

Maimonides was born in Cordova, Spain, in the very last days of Moorish rule. His father was a distinguished rabbi and physician who traced his lineage back through many generations of learned persons. Little is known about Maimonides's mother, who may have died in childbirth. As a youngster he received a thorough education. But in 1148, the fanatical Islamic sect of the Almohades conquered the entire region from their base in Morocco. Their bloody slogans were "No church and no synagogue" and "Death to the infidels!" Faced with the choice of apostasy or death, Maimonides and his family, like many other Jews, were forced into a weary exile. For nearly twelve years they wandered across Spain, and spent a dispiriting half-decade in Fez, Morocco. In 1165 they journeyed once more, briefly, to the Land of Israel, and finally settled in Fostat, near Cairo.

During this outwardly unstable period in Maimonides's life, he managed to maintain his education and scholarly interests. By the time he was twenty-three, he had already written two books that revealed his immense talent for methodical thinking. The first was a treatise on the complexities of the lunar-based Hebrew calendar; the second was an introduction to Greek logic. A man of diverse intellectual interests, he began to write his *Commentary on the Mishnah* while simultaneously studying medicine under some of the leading theorists in the Arabic world.

Once settled in Cairo, Maimonides swiftly rose to prominence as a scholar of Jewish studies. His *Commentary*, rich with an emphasis on ethics as the basis for Jewish law, catapulted him to widespread attention; like many of his other works, it is still studied today. Before long, Maimonides's co-religionists elevated him to rabbi and communal leader, posts for which he refused any material compensation. As his reputation as an authority on Jewish affairs grew steadily, Jews from far-flung communities all over the globe sought him out in person or wrote him letters for advice on religious, social, and political matters. He busily composed appropriate *Responsa* and gave counsel when asked; he also found time to start his *Mishneh Torah* (*Code of Maimonides*), which would become a definitive guide to the Talmud for centuries to come.

But tragedy befell Maimonides in 1174, when his brother David was drowned in a shipwreck. With him was lost the entire family fortune, in the form of jewels he had been carrying for trade. David, a successful jewel merchant, had willingly supported his brother's family as well as his own; the two men had been extremely close to one another. Grief-stricken, Maimonides was now obligated to shoulder a host of unfamiliar financial responsibilities; his scholastic and communal activities would have to make room for economic considerations. And so, Maimonides embarked on a new career as a practicing physician. True to his character, he applied to this seemingly secular discipline his same qualities of meticulous scholarship and spiritual sensitivity.

Over the next few years, Maimonides's reputation as a healer blossomed. He regarded his profession as a sacred duty, one which required unstinting devotion. Thus he zealously kept abreast of all the latest medical discoveries and critically examined the great medical texts of the past. Rejecting the popular belief in amulets and magical potions as forms of cure, Maimonides insisted that treatment of illness demands a comprehensive knowledge of the human mind and body. In contrast to many of his medical colleagues, he downplayed the significance of drugs and surgery, and argued that diet, exercise, and mental outlook are the key determinants of health. He related various physical ailments, including asthma and digestive disorders, to specific emotional imbalances such as chronic anxiety, anger, and depression.

Not surprisingly, Maimonides's bold and creative approach to healing eventually attracted the notice of the royal family in nearby Cairo. In 1185, he became court physician to the Grand Vizier Alfadhel, and later to the Sultan Saladin himself. Maimonides served with great fame in this capacity; so much so, in fact, that King Richard the Lion-Hearted of England asked him to become his personal physician. Maimonides, however, preferred to remain with the Jewish community in Egypt and declined the offer. It is fascinating to speculate how subsequent Jewish history—and Western history as a whole—might have changed had Maimonides accepted this lofty position in London.

Although dedicated to his burgeoning medical practice, Maimonides also continued his active philosophical and religious involvements. In 1180, he completed his *Mishneh Torah*, which brought him additional prominence in the Jewish world. This work was noteworthy for its fusion of Jewish law and philosophy, as well as for its all-encompassing scope. A decade later, Maimonides completed *The Guide for the Perplexed*, undoubtedly his best-known and most influential volume. It represented his effort to synthesize Greek and Jewish thought in his search for ultimate truth. Incorporating many realms of intellectual discourse, *The Guide* also set forth specific principles on how each of us can attain higher states of consciousness. Though Maimonides was certainly a rationalist by the standards of his own time, he believed strongly in the reality of realms beyond our mundane perceptions. For example, in *The Guide* he declared, ''If a person, perfect in his intellectual and moral faculties, and also perfect, as far as possible, in his imaginative faculty, prepares himself [properly] . . . he must become a prophet, for prophecy is a natural state of man.''

Maimonides maintained an extremely demanding personal schedule in his last years. In a famous and vivid letter to the translator of *The Guide*, Rabbi Samuel ibn Tibbon, Maimonides commented,

My duties to the Sultan are very heavy. I am obliged to visit him every day, early in the morning. When he or any of his children, or any of the inmates in his harem, are indisposed, I dare not quit . . . [When I return home], I find the antechamber filled with people, both Jews and Gentiles, nobles and common people . . . patients go in and out until nightfall, and sometimes even [later] . . . When night falls, I am so exhausted I can scarcely speak.

Maimonides kept up this unflagging daily pace, coupled with his active scholarly and communal activities, until his death in 1204 at the age of sixty-nine. His books on philosophy and health became classics for people of all faiths and backgrounds. His insights on Jewish law and ethics have exerted a tremendous influence for centuries. As the popular rabbinic saying has long declared, "From the time of Moses the prophet to the time of Moses Maimonides, there has arisen none like this Moses."

Maimonides's perspective on inner development is difficult to summarize succintly, for he advanced his views in many diverse religious and medical writings. Indeed, Maimonides regarded his advice on physical health to be intimately related to his spiritual and ethical formulations. In essence, he emphasized that without proper care for our bodies, we are unable to awaken our higher mental capabilities. Nor, he insisted, can we fully appreciate the divine splendor of the universe if we are ill or weak. "One should aim to maintain physical health and vigor, in order that his soul may be upright, in a condition to know God," Maimonides observed. "For it is impossible for one to understand sciences and meditate upon them when he is hungry or sick, or when any of his limbs is aching."

In such farsighted works as *The Preservation of Youth*, Maimonides therefore prescribed a variety of methods for attaining bodily vitality. He viewed diet as extremely important and delineated in considerable detail which foods should be eaten separately or in certain combinations. He regarded vigorous daily exercise as essential to our total well-being—and suggested that it be continued to the point when we feel a warm, energy-like flow within us. Intriguingly, Maimonides also recommended—within the context of marriage—that lovemaking be valued for its beneficial effects on our overall health. Stressing that true vigor depends upon regular, sound habits, he declared that, "Whoever lives in accordance with the directions I have set forth has my assurance that he will never be sick until he grows old . . . he will not be in need of a physician, and will enjoy excellent health as long as he lives."

Like other great healers throughout history, Maimonides possessed an acute understanding of the emotional factors in health and illness. In many of his writings on Jewish law and ethics, he pinpointed chronic anger and depression as particularly harmful in their physical effects. Thus he advised that each of us should engage in regular self-examination and study of sacred works such as *Pirkey Avoth*—to develop powerful inner resources.

"It is well known that emotions of the soul affect the body and produce great, significant, and wide-ranging changes in the state of health," Maimonides stated. "Emotions of the soul should be watched, regularly examined, and kept well-balanced."

To those distressed by anxiety, depression, or other forms of emotional disturbance, Maimonides offered specific guidance. For example, he recommended—consistent with longstanding Jewish belief—that music and song be utilized for therapeutic purposes. "One suffering from melancholia," he stated, "may rid himself of it by listening to singing and all kinds of instrumental music, by strolling through beautiful gardens and splendid buildings, by gazing upon beautiful pictures, and other things that enliven the mind, and dissipate gloomy moods. The purpose of all this is to restore the healthful conditions of the body [and] . . . to acquire wisdom."

Maimonides further expounded that once we have attained true physical and emotional vibrancy, then we become able to experience higher, prophetic states of consciousness. Mental and bodily weaknesses hinder such growth, he felt; hence his emphasis on eliminating such shortcomings from our being. Maimonides taught that we must cultivate our powers of imagination to gain entry into loftier realms of awareness—for the supernal worlds are beyond our ordinary sensations. In *The Guide*, he succinctly commented,

Part of the function of the imaginative faculty is . . . to retain sensory impressions, to combine them, and chiefly to form images. [However] . . . the principal and highest function is performed when the senses are at rest in their action, for then it receives, to some extent, divine inspiration . . . this is the nature of dreams which prove true and also of prophecy.

Maimonides's approach to our inner world was extremely comprehensive and unparalleled in its influence during medieval and later Judaism. He was convinced that when we achieve genuine bodily vigor, fully master our emotions through consistent self-examination, and free our imagination from petty tensions and desires—then the celestial gates swing open before us. In an unequivocal message of optimism that has inspired countless men and women of all traditions, Maimonides declared, "One who satisfies these conditions—such a person will undoubtedly perceive only things very extraordinary and divine."

## Kabbalah: The Way of Splendor

While the rationalist philosophers sought logical principles to understand our inner world, other Jewish thinkers pursued the intuitive wisdom of the mystical path. For much of the modern era academicians contemptuously dismissed this aspect of Judaism as largely an aberration; but it is now unmistakably clear that some of the greatest figures in Jewish history have been ardent mystics. Thanks in part to the impeccable scholarship of Gershom Scholem and his colleagues at the Hebrew University in Israel, the true creative genius of Judaism's esoteric system has become increasingly apparent. It would be no exaggeration to say that, for growing numbers of men and women around the globe, the mystical perspective represents the most alluring feature of age-old Jewish thought.

The Jewish mystical approach is generally known as the Kabbalah, from the Hebrew root-word ''to receive.'' Underlying this term have long been the twin notions that this sacred knowledge was originally received through divine illumination, and then transmitted intact from one generation's spiritual masters to the next. Scholarly research indicates that as far back as the time of Rabbi Akiba in the second century C.E.—and possibly even centuries earlier, to the biblical Prophets—esoteric doctrines and practices have been vital to Judaism. It is equally true that for the major portions of Jewish history, this tradition has been essentially oral and secret in nature. Its adepts strongly warned against idle dabbling into this arcane system of knowledge, for they believed it to be quite harmful in the hands of the untutored—potentially leading even to madness or death.

The earliest known elements of Jewish mysticism are mentioned only briefly, and with caution, in the Talmud. They are identified as *Ma'aseh Bereshith* (*Act of Creation*) and *Ma'aseh Merkabah* (*Act of the Divine Chariot*). The former seems to have comprised abstruse metaphysical speculation related to the creation of the cosmos, and the nature of space and time; the latter embodied specific, experiential methods for attaining transcendent realms of awareness. Little concrete information is available regarding either of these disciplines, though fragmentary writings that have survived intimate that special bodily postures, rhythmic chanting of Hebrew prayers, and variant modes of breathing were utilized to propel initiates into altered states of consciousness.

The first Jewish metaphysical text to appear was the *Sefer Yetzirah* (*Book of Creation*). It originated anonymously in the Middle East, between the third and sixth centuries C.E. Composed in an extremely terse style, it constitutes less than two thousand words in its entirety. In fact, the *Sefer Yetzirah* resembles in format a summary or outline of mystical doctrines, presumably elaborated elsewhere through oral means. Its major theme is that the letters of the Hebrew alphabet represent visual and auditory patterns of energy by which the universe was created—and continues to be sustained.

By adding the twenty-two Hebrew letters to the ten primordial numbers—*sefirot*, or energy-essences, as they are termed—the *Sefer Yetzirah* delineates that thirty-two secret routes to the deity exist in the cosmos. All aspects of space, time, and our relation to them are said to be upheld by the never-ending interplay of these vibrational forces.

"In thirty-two mysterious paths of wisdom did God decree . . . He created his Universe with three numerations: Number, Speech, and Writing," declares the *Book of Creation*. And then, with apparent reference to meditation, it instructs, "Know, think, and visualize. Ponder deeply and seat the Creator in His place."

Despite its brevity, the *Sefer Yetzirah* served as the foundation for Jewish esoteric speculation and practice for hundreds of years. Indeed, it was not until more than a half-millennium that the next key text of Jewish mysticism appeared. Entitled the *Sefer Bahir* (*Book of Brilliance*), it first surfaced in Provence, southern France, around the year 1175. Because of its relatively detailed and precise formulations, the *Bahir* is viewed by modern scholars as the beginning of the formal, kabbalistic era of Jewish history. The central thesis of this evocative and complex volume is that there lies a vast and unseen order beyond what we ordinarily perceive in everyday life. Through our diligent self-development, we are told, the divine splendor gradually becomes more accessible to us; meditation is prized as a sacred activity to achieve this exalted, inner condition.

Perhaps reflecting, too, the oppressed situation of European Jewry in the Middle Ages, these early kabbalists emphasized the hidden aspects of the deity. "People want to see the King," the *Bahir* observes, "but do not know where to find his house. First, they [must] ask, 'Where is the King's house?' Only then can they ask, 'Where is the King?'''

Interestingly, the *Bahir* also advances the notion of reincarnation—the first recorded instance of Jewish belief in this intriguing subject. In addition, the *Bahir* articulates the concept that a subtle ''life-energy'' flows throughout the human body; this current is seen to underlie our mental and physical health through certain energy-bodies or *sefirot* within us. Both of these esoteric doctrines became central to later mystical writings in Judaism.

Valued as both a metaphysical treatise and a practical manual for reaching the inner Source, the *Bahir* spread rapidly throughout the Jewish world. For the first time, mystical ideas about self-growth began to find a wider audience among Jews. Especially in southern France and Spain, the kabbalists started to acquire a distinct religious identity. At roughly the same historical period, a somewhat parallel development occurred among North European Jewry, centered in Germany. Known as the Hasidim (Pious), and not to be confused with their Eastern European namesakes of the eighteenth century, these adepts stressed bodily self-denial and strict emotional self-control as the surest path to transcendence of mundane existence. They also made use of sustained fasting, dream exploration, and prolonged meditation as techniques for personal advancement.

Toward the end of the thirteenth century, Jewish mysticism expanded considerably in influence. The most important forces for this change were undoubtedly Abraham ben Samuel Abulafia (c. 1240-1292) and the *Zohar* (*Book of Splendor*) respectively. Each exerted a tremendous impact on the promulgation of esoteric speculation and practice among world Jewry. To the present day, each continues to inspire Jews drawn to the path of spiritual growth.

Born in Sargossa, Spain, Abulafia became drawn at an early age to the writings of Maimonides, as well as to the Kabbalah. With an iconclastic and forceful personality, Abulafia was not interested in preparing for conventional rabbinical work; he preferred to remain a lay teacher of the mystical tradition and travel throughout the Mediterranean region. On more than one occasion he provoked the wrath of the rabbinical establishment, as he insisted that the possibility of divine revelation exists for all. But he strongly rejected the charge that he was a heretic.

''God knows and the people of Israel know that, with my limited knowledge of the Torah, I am not moved by sinister motives,'' Abulafia declared. ''I am inspired to take this step [because] . . . of the lack of people knowledgeable in the wisdom of the Kabbalah in our time.''

In keeping with Maimonides's approach to our inner potential, Abulafia argued that we each have the latent capacity to achieve exalted states of consciousness, even that of prophecy. ''Prophets begin by being illuminated with the light of life,'' Abulafia wrote in one of his many meditative guides, ''and from this stage, they rise from light to light through meditation. Through the enhancement of their merit, they approach the highest distinction to a point where the speech they hear within themselves is linked to the Fountain from which all speech derives.''

Abulafia's most enduring legacy to the mystical tradition of Judaism was his concrete method for attaining heightened realms of awareness. Consistent with the age-old teachings of the *Sefer Yetzirah*, he developed a complex and immensely powerful system of meditation based on the letters of the Hebrew alphabet—a system still practiced today in Israel and elsewhere. ''Concentrate on all of [the letters],'' he instructed, ''in all their aspects, like a person who is told a parable, or a riddle, or a dream, or as one who ponders a book of wisdom.'' As part of Abulafia's complete orientation to higher development, he also prescribed yoga-like bodily postures, exotic breathing techniques, and solitary contemplation as pathways to the divine.

Even more influential than Abraham Abulafia on subsequent Jewish esotericism has been the *Zohar*. It first appeared in late-thirteenth-century Spain, and is unquestionably the most important and authoritative work in Judaism's entire mystical tradition. For many centuries, Jews and non-Jews alike have regarded this deeply symbolic and poetic text as a sacred communication from above. Written anonymously in a lofty style of Aramaic, the *Zohar*'s very language and imagery is said to transform our ordinary view of the world. Though traditionalists ascribe the *Zohar* to Rabbi Simon bar Yochai of the second century C.E., most scholars today attribute it to Rabbi Moses de Leon, a prominent kabbalist in his own era.

The *Zohar* is multi-tiered in layers of meaning, and defies simple analysis. Stylistically, its format mainly records the abstruse conversations purported to have taken place among Rabbi Simon bar Yochai, his son Eliezer, and other holy sages as they traveled about the Land of Israel in the decades after the Temple of Jerusalem was destroyed. Yet, the tone of their remarks is never one of gloom, but rather of exaltation concerning the "myriad worlds upon worlds by which the Holy One makes His glory known."

The *Zohar*'s mood is often dream-like; flying scrolls materialize out of thin air and then disappear; hidden caves are revealed to hold secret, angelic manuscripts; seemingly ignorant folk or even children suddenly utter cryptic statements that explain arcane mysteries of the universe. The *Zohar* is also replete with highly erotic imagery, for its anonymous author saw the act of human lovemaking as a mirror of the divine and ecstatic process of celestial creation.

In essence, the *Zohar* tells us that we walk through daily life as though asleep. We are seen to be oblivious to the countless spheres of supernal radiance that surround us at all times. Thus, this sacred work declares that, "Man, whilst in this world, considers not and reflects not what he is standing on, and each day as it passes, he regards as though it has vanished into nothingness." But with increased discernment, we are informed, each of us is capable of perceiving the hidden connections that permeate the cosmos.

Paralleling the notions of modern quantum physics, the *Zohar* affirms repeatedly that everything in the universe is linked to everything else; nothing exists in true isolation from the whole. Thus the more we comprehend about the nature of Creation, the broader our understanding of the world within. "As man's body consists of members and parts of various ranks, all acting and reacting upon each other so as to form one organism," explains the *Zohar* "so does the world at large consist of a hierarchy of created things, which when they properly act and react upon each together, form literally one organic body."

Filled with allusions to dreams, meditation, altered states of awareness, the mind-body relationship, extra-sensory perception, and life-after-death, the *Zohar* has since its appearance strongly influenced esoteric psychology in the West. As it circulated throughout Europe in the fourteenth and fifteenth centuries, it gained many adherents. Jewish commentaries on it were developed in many countries; Catholic theologians too found some of its exotic notions about the deity to be quite intriguing. But it was not until the mid-sixteenth century that the Kabbalah flowered into its most magnificent and universal form.

The catalyzing event was the Spanish Expulsion of Jews in the year 1492; shortly thereafter, for mainly political reasons, the Portuguese royalty banished all of its Jewish citizens. In both nations, those who remained faced certain torture and death. Thousands of Jews were forced to seek refuge in North Africa, the Near East, and other unfamiliar places; some eventually made their way to the Holy Land, a poor and backward region. There, in the small town of Safed, those drawn to the mystical path began to congregate. With no end in sight for the Great Exile itself, and political action unthinkable, some Jews now found quite alluring the personal transcendence long promised by the Kabbalah. Moreover, some felt compelled to discover hidden meaning in the tragedy of the Spanish Expulsion and other Jewish suffering in their times.

In the second half of the sixteenth century, several of the most important mystics of all Jewish history lived and associated with one another in Safed. The most significant figure was Rabbi Isaac Luria (1534–1572), whose parents were originally of European origin. Known as the Ari (in Hebrew, *ari* means lion; but it is also an acronym for his title, the Ashkenazi Rabbi Isaac), he became revered in his own lifetime as a saint and a seer nearly unequaled in Jewish annals. The visionary power of the Ari's ideas—he wrote no books and transmitted his compelling teachings almost entirely through oral means—raised the Kabbalah to the loftiest and most venerated realms of Judaism.

Luria's central message addressed the very basis of human existence. He elaborated a theosophy describing a cosmic sequence of events by which the universe was created—and vividly accounted for the nature of good and evil, life and death, free will and the soul. In his bold system of thought, God withdrew a portion of His glory so that matter could come into being. In a sense, this inconceivable act created a "space" and left "fallen" shards of the divine lodged in all living and non-living forms in the cosmos.

In Luria's intriguing view, each of us thus has a special mission or destiny: to elevate these sparks in our own lives, back to their original Source; every soul has its unique tasks to accomplish. Through our deeds, words, and even innermost thoughts, we are said to possess the power to aid in this radiant process of *tikkun* (rectification, or redemption).

Luria went on to emphasize the importance of our intentionality and will (*kavvanah*). He taught that with the properly developed inner focus, we can move whole worlds above. But lacking that strength of being, we are ultimately little more potent than the dumb beasts that walk the fields. To help his followers acquire true *kavvanah*, the Ari devised a variety of complex, rigorous techniques of meditation and concentration. These especially involved detailed visualizations of the ten *sefirot* and the kabbalistic Tree of Life.

Luria's exciting ideas traveled with both rapidity and considerable impact throughout the Jewish world. His devoted disciples carried his system to far-off countries—initially Turkey and the Near East, then to Italy, Holland, Germany, and eventually to Poland and Eastern Europe. Though the theosophical and metaphysical subtleties of his thought exceeded the grasp of most unlearned Jewry, his alluring outlook inspired new generations of religious writers and poets. In this way, Lurianic Kabbalah penetrated many spheres of mainstream Judaism, including law, ethics, and moralistic discourse.

Then, in the 1660's, a disastrous messianic movement based loosely on kabbalistic concepts erupted in the Near East. Led by Sabbatai Zevi and his disciple Nathan of Gaza, it inflamed Jewish hopes that their long, long Exile was about to end. Thousands of Jews, encompassing those in distant lands, abandoned their livelihoods and homes to await the imminent coming of the Day of Judgment. The debacle ended with Sabbatai Zevi's forced conversion to Islam and the shattering of much renewed religious enthusiasm. Rabbinical leaders thereupon decided that the mystical tradition was simply too explosive in the hands of the untutored and forbade its study to all but the most well-schooled of Jews.

### Hasidism: Raising the Holy Sparks

Since its very origins in the ancient past, the Jewish mystical tradition had inspired many individual seekers with its evocative ideas. They regarded its exalted doctrines with the highest veneration. Yet, kabbalistic insights concerning personal growth remained limited, by and large, to a small number of Jews in each generation—that is, until the advent of the Hasidic (meaning "pious") movement in eighteenth- and early nineteenth-century Eastern Europe. Extolling the everyday world as the doorway to the divine, the early Hasidic leaders specifically addressed the issue of how we can achieve greater joy and transcendence in life. Perhaps precisely because classic Hasidism so clearly emphasized the elevation of our inner traits, it has undergone a tremendous revival of interest in recent years. To those at least nominally familiar with other mystical paths, Hasidic teachings seem to exert special attraction.

Within the relatively brief historical span of some seventy-five years, Hasidism arose from the charistmatic fervor of one man— Israel ben Eliezer (c. 1698–1760)—to be fully embraced by half the Jews of Poland and Russia; these were the major concentrations of world Jewry at the time. The Hasidic outlook was one of optimism and hope; its founder and the many disciples he led stressed that sheer brilliance of scholarship is ultimately useless unless it touches the heart. Each of us is capable of reaching the highest supernal realms through joyous devotion, they taught; our intellectual and social attainments are secondary.

"No child can be born except through pleasure and joy," Israel ben Eliezer is credited with saying. "By the same token, if one wishes for his prayers to bear fruit, he must offer them with pleasure and joy." To a people long oppressed and impoverished in a hostile Gentile world, the Hasidic message of religious passion spread like a holy fire across the village landscape.

Ironically, almost nothing is known for sure about the founder of Hasidism himself. In his own day he became popularly known as the Baal Shem Tov ("Master of the Good Name," or "Besht" in abbreviation), due to his fame as a "miracle-worker." Though legends arose about him even during his lifetime, scholars today generally agree that Israel was born in the small *shtetl* of Okup, near the Carpathian mountains. He came from a family distinguished neither by education nor economic position. Israel's parents died when he was young, and apparently someone from the community took him in and raised him. For several years, Israel served as a teacher's aide—a duty low in status—and transported the children to and from the synagogue school. Seemingly unrefined and ignorant, Israel initially so disgusted his brother-in-law, a prominent rabbi, that he urged his sister to divorce him. But she refused to do so and the couple moved away to a far-off village in the Carpathian mountains. There they eked out a living close to nature, and later ran an inn in the town of Medzyboz.

During this period, Israel ben Eliezer gradually developed a reputation as a healer and "wonder-worker." According to legend, he first revealed his spiritual mastery to the world at the age of thirty-six, in about 1734. We are told that he demonstrated vast knowledge of the Kabbalah and was thereby able to perform uncanny acts to help others in need. Traveling from village to village, the Baal Shem Tov cured those sick or in despair. He typically made use of spiritual counseling, laying-on-of-hands, and herbal remedies in his treatment. More importantly, he also transmitted a unique and alluring approach to Judaism.

Relying largely on the technique of folktales and parables, the Besht expounded abstruse mystical notions in simple language that tens of thousands could readily understand. Few Jews could command the economic resources necessary to devote years of quiet study to the *Zohar* and other arcane texts. In essence, he took classic kabbalistic themes about the nature of human existence and our relation to the divine, and cast these in the form of compelling stories. His central notion—at the heart of Luria's system—was that every individual has a specific mission to carry out in fulfilling his or her purpose on earth.

"No two persons have the same abilities," the Baal Shem Tov declared. "Each man should work in the service of God according to his own talents. If one man tries to imitate another, he merely loses the opportunity to do good through his own merit."

Although the Besht drew his early followers predominantly from the ranks of the poor and unlearned, he eventually began to attract some of the leading Talmudic scholars of the time. Some held positions of high influence and leadership within the Jewish communities of Eastern Europe. Though he was only a lay preacher, they were quite impressed with his mastery of mystical lore and his pious yet magnetic personality. Legend has it that, on many occasions, the Baal Shem Tov demonstrated such paranormal powers as telepathy, clairvoyance, and precognition. Several years before his death in 1760, he carefully chose certain disciples to succeed him in promulgating the Hasidic message. Many of them became brilliant spiritual teachers in their own right and established particular followings. Indeed, in its first half-century of growth, Hasidism generated its greatest creative energy and produced a galaxy of remarkable leaders.

The direct heir to the Baal Shem Tov's position was Rabbi Dov Baer of Mezritch (1710–1772). Known as the Maggid (spiritual master), he was well known early in his life as an incisive but overly ascetic scholar, drawn to the contemplative mysteries of the Kabbalah. Curious as to the validity of the reports circulating about the Besht, Rabbi Dov Baer (according to tradition) sought him out and challenged him to explain a difficult portion of the *Zohar*. After first hearing Rabbi Dov Baer's analysis of the passage, the Hasidic founder offered his viewpoint. As he did so, the dazzle of celestial beings reputedly filled the room. "Your interpretation was correct," the Besht quietly said to the astonished ascetic, "but your way of study lacks soul." Thereupon, Rabbi Dov Baer became won over to the Baal Shem Tov's more joyful, exuberant approach to life.

The Maggid cogently systematized much of his mentor's teachings. Like the Besht, he insisted that our normal state of awareness resembles that of sleep. To truly perceive the supernal glory that surrounds us, we must strip away our egoistic desires, he explained, "so that the divine energy [within] will be of infinite greatness." Rabbi Dov Baer also methodically organized the spread of Hasidism to initially apathetic or unfriendly Jewish communities in Eastern Europe. For some Jews—known as *Mitnaggedim* ("Opponents")—viewed with disdain and even alarm the Hasidic rejection of Talmudic study as the sole path to saintliness. Especially in the Lithuanian region, rabbinical opposition to Hasidism was fierce and protracted. Hasidic adherents were publicly excommunicated and their writings burned as heresy. However, Rabbi Dov Baer's diligent organizing efforts continued unabated, gaining new allies and supporters with each passing year.

As Hasidism found itself more securely established with age, it began to lose some of its revolutionary zeal, perhaps inevitably so. Thus some Hasidic leaders started to downplay the importance of the Baal Shem Tov's methods for achieving self-transcendence; they quietly abandoned his meditative techniques and styles of prayer. The simple passage of time also exerted its effects. To new generations of Jews, the Besht and his original associates were no longer real, flesh-and-blood individuals, but historically distant and, increasingly, superhuman and mythic figures.

Of course, many in the Hasidic movement sensed with dismay the spiritual decline occurring around them. One of the greatest of such personages who sought to rekindle the initial flame was Rabbi Schneur Zalman of Liady (1747–1812). He became the founder of the Lubavitcher Hasidim—a group that still flourishes and embraces the mystical aspects of Judaism. Born in central Russia, Rabbi Schneur Zalman was a child prodigy in his mastery of the Talmud. When he was ready for advanced scholarship, he chose to become a disciple of the Maggid of Mezritch, who had already engendered controversy for his allegiance to the Baal Shem Tov. The Maggid encouraged his gifted young student—more than thirty-five years his junior—to develop his metaphysical and theosophical interests within the mystical, experiential sphere of Hasidism. The culmination of Rabbi Schneur Zalman's intellectual work was his book, the *Tanya* (It Has Been Taught), an abstract but provocative treatise studied extensively to this day by Lubavitcher Hasidim and others.

In the *Tanya*, Rabbi Schneur Zalman taught that it is a basic human desire to merge with the Infinite or *Ein Sof*. In describing our inborn longing for the deity, he emphasized that each soul "naturally yearns to separate itself and depart from the body, in order to unify with its origin and Source . . . the fountainhead of all life." But he viewed the process of self-development toward the divine as one that requires lifelong devotion and the appropriate use of both intellect and emotion.

Amidst bitter opposition from the non-Hasidic rabbinic establishment, Rabbi Schneur Zalman promulgated meditative practices designed to help people attain closer communion with the Holy One. His foes condemned such ideas as heresy. Twice, on rumors instigated by the *Mitnaggedim*, Rabbi Schneur Zalman was imprisoned by the Czar for allegedly fomenting subversion. Though his situation was perilous, he was released unharmed on both occasions, due to lack of evidence and his own unbending will. After his second release, in 1801, it was clear even to his antagonists that he was not going to stop preaching and that the Hasidic movement could not be destroyed. With superb organizational skills, Rabbi Schneur Zalman made sure that the Lubavitchers would long remain unified—and, indeed, they have been so for nearly two centuries.

Another spiritual giant of this era was Rabbi Nachman of Bratslav (1772–1810). Among many Jews today, his name has come to be associated with the heights of Hasidic spirituality. As the great-grandson of the Baal Shem Tov, Nachman from childhood was regarded as destined to be an important leader of the Hasidim. At an early age, he became drawn to the beauty of nature as a manifestation of the divine, and spent long hours in solitary prayer and meditation outdoors. While still in his teens, he began to experience visions and present talks on the means to higher consciousness.

Rabbi Nachman's ideas were bold and unorthodox, for he stressed personal dialogue with God and meditation as essential for climbing the exalted ladder within. He insisted that each of his followers devote at least an hour per day to their individual spiritual needs and declared that, "If you set aside a time each day to converse with God, you will surely be worthy of finding Him." He also prescribed a variety of specific meditative techniques for overcoming the pull of the mundane in everyday existence; many of these are based on an extremely sophisticated understanding of our emotions and their relation to both spirit and body. An inherent optimist, Rabbi Nachman often taught that, "Man includes all the worlds. There is nothing beyond his ability."

Though Rabbi Nachman of Bratslav attracted a fervently loyal following, his iconoclasm led to inevitable friction with the Hasidic establishment; by the early 1800s, it had become progressively more conservative and rigid in its own way. He also encountered the inevitable difficulty of attempting to describe by rational means the nature of mystical or transcendent experience:

"You may have a vision, but even with yourself, you cannot share it. Today, you may be inspired to see a new light. But tomorrow, you will no longer be able to communicate it—even to yourself.

Thus, several years before Rabbi Nachman's death from tuberculosis at the age of thirty-eight, he began to tell stories to his flock. "People may be asleep all their lives," he observed, "but through tales told by a true *zaddik* [holy one], they can be awakened." He believed that such methods may truly effect changes inside ourselves, while more intellectual approaches can be easily blocked by our egos. For this reason, Rabbi Nachman also prized music as a pathway to the divine—and composed many songs to this end.

Dazzling in their poetic imagery and symbolic beauty, Rabbi Nachman's surrealist stories have as their themes classic kabbalistic concepts about the human condition; yet, because they operate simultaneously on many levels of meaning, they defy purely rational analysis. In the world of Rabbi Nachman's tales, exiled kings and lost princesses, hidden treasures and stormy seas, undaunted heroes and saintly beggars, shipwrecked sailors, and madmen all represent in some way our situation on earth. Most of the stories were recorded in an obviously garbled manner, for their author did not write any of them down. In 1815, thirteen of these were published posthumously in Yiddish with a Hebrew translation; in recent years, several evocative retellings have appeared in English. Following Rabbi Nachman's statement—"My light will glow till the days of the Messiah"—Bratslaver Hasidim still speak of their founder in the present tense and have never appointed a successor to his spiritual mission.

### *Musar* and the Search for Character

The last psychologically innovative movement to have arisen within the context of traditional Judaism is that of *musar* (ethics). It originated in Lithuania, the bastion of talmudic study in the middle decades of the nineteenth-century, and reached its pinnacle of influence in Eastern Europe just before the enormous wave of Jewish migration to the United States took place. Because only a few *musar* texts have been translated into English, this intriguing approach to self-development has remained relatively unknown outside of the Hebrew-speaking world. Yet, in recent years, *musar* has become the focus of increasing interest among many Jews; the accessibility of concrete information on this topic will no doubt help determine its impact on the contemporary, Jewish spiritual renewal.

Though the *musar* movement certainly possessed its own historically unique features, it resembled early Hasidism in two significant respects. First, *musar* teachings were specifically promulgated to effect a radical, inner awakening among Jews in the modern world. That is, the exponents of this psycho-ethical system sought to regenerate a true Jewish spirituality in which individuals could once again feel close to the divine in everyday life. Like the Hasidic founders, *musar* advocates viewed this issue as indeed central to the future of Judaism.

Second, the growth of *musar*, similar to its Hasidic counterpart about a century earlier, can be directly traced to the dedication of one charismatic figure: Rabbi Israel (Lipkin) Salanter. Over the course of his energetic lifetime, he succeeded in bringing to tens of thousands his inspiring perspective on personal growth.

It should be noted at the outset that the *musar* approach was never as pervasive in its influence as early Hasidism; nor did Rabbi Salanter ever attain the legendary and almost celestial status of the Baal Shem Tov. Indeed, *musar* partly arose to negate the tendency to excessive hero (or *zaddik*) worship so prevalent in the Hasidic milieu. Perhaps *musar* never achieved the impact of Hasidism because of very different historical circumstances of world Jewry by the middle nineteenth century; European liberalism and political democracy had become important forces by that time. No doubt, too, in its very emphasis on methodical self-development, *musar* was not composed of the material that gives rise to sweeping mass movements.

Israel Lipkin was born in Zagory, Lithuania, in 1810. His father was a well-known Jewish scholar; his mother was also reportedly quite knowledgeable about the ritual observances. At a young age, Israel demonstrated keen intellectual prowess. Around the age of nine, his father sent him to the Lithuanian town of Salant to study the Talmud intensively. There the lad became a pupil of Rabbi Joseph Zundel, an inspiring figure who emphasized ethical concepts within the talmudic context. Israel associated closely with Rabbi Zundel for fifteen years, until the latter emigrated to the Holy Land.

Following the departure of his mentor, Rabbi Israel Salanter (as he came to be known) began to travel as an itinerant teacher throughout the villages of Lithuania. He possessed obvious erudition, combined with a forceful yet warm personality. Not surprisingly, he attracted considerable attention wherever he went. By 1840, he had so distinguished himself that he was asked to direct one of the leading talmudic academies in Vilna, the world center of Jewish religious thought. For a young man of thirty, such a post was almost unprecedented.

For the next seven years, Rabbi Salanter developed and promulgated the basic elements of his unique *musar* system. He preferred to devote the bulk of his time to original scholarship, and left his position as dean after only two years to teach instead at a small seminary on Vilna's outskirts. Quite deliberately, he sought to advance his innovative doctrine of character development as the basis for a new movement within Judaism. His vision was of a revitalized Jewish spirituality for the modern age—a faith that remained true to traditional practice but incorporated the best features of the scientific outlook. Rabbi Salanter insisted that if such a celebrated Jew as Maimonides could achieve this synthesis in the Middle Ages, contemporary Jews could do likewise.

In 1848, Rabbi Salanter gained widespread attention—and controversy—for his activity in another realm: social welfare and relief work. A devastating epidemic of plague and cholera swept through the impoverished Jewish and Gentile communities of Lithuania. Thousands died, including many children. Rabbi Salanter tirelessly organized committees of aid for the stricken and their families. As the High Holy Days approached, he urged his fellow ailing Jews *not* to refrain from eating and drinking on Yom Kippur; to perform the usual abstinence would in this case constitute the overriding sin of refusing the divine gift of life itself, he declared. Thereupon, to dramatize his point, Rabbi Salanter led Yom Kippur services and passed out cookies and wine to his congregants. This heartfelt but iconclastic act alienated him from some of his older, more cautious colleagues.

The following year, Rabbi Salanter moved to the town of Kovno in Lithuania. He wished to avoid some of the trappings of fame that had begun to surround him, especially after he discovered that Czarist leaders were seeking to lure him to direct an assimilationist school they were hoping to establish for Jews in the region. In his refusal to collaborate with the Czarist officials, Rabbi Salanter clearly indicated his own stance with respect to Jewish self-identity in the Gentile world; beyond a certain line, he argued, to compromise with secularism was tantamount to religious suicide.

In Kovno, Rabbi Salanter established his own seminary and further developed his *musar* philosophy and method. During this period, he influenced many *yeshiva* students, who later matured into articulate rabbinical advocates for his approach. As an educational administrator as well as a theoretician, Rabbi Salanter was never content merely to lecture about spiritual psychology; he felt obligated to wed ideas to action. Indeed, a basic aspect of his entire orientation was that, in day-to-day life, it is our deeds that really matter, not simply our good intentions.

In an illustrative episode of this period, Rabbi Salanter once found a *yeshiva* student bedridden due to illness. Rabbi Salanter asked the people who prayed in the young man's synagogue, "Why aren't you taking better care of him?"

"Our community doesn't have any money," they replied.

Rabbi Salanter then screamed at them, "You should have sold the fancy cover on the ark in which the Torah scrolls are kept, and used the money to help this person!"

Rabbi Salanter seemed to be quite angry, but someone overheard him whisper to himself, "External anger only. External anger only."

In 1857, after nine successful years in Kovno, the *musar* founder startled many of his more conventional colleagues when he took up residence in Germany, following a brief treatment there for health problems. Germany was the worldwide stronghold of Jewish assimilation; it is estimated, for example, that approximately one-quarter of Berlin's Jews converted to Catholicism in the early decades of the nineteenth century. Many of Rabbi Salanter's associates felt he was abandoning his mission of piety by deciding to relocate away from his supporters; but his goal was to strike at the very heart of the assimilationist forces by offering an exciting alternative to mainstream Jewish Orthodoxy of the day.

Rabbi Salanter maintained his German residence until his death in 1883, though he frequently returned to Lithuania for extended periods of time; several of his last years were also spent in Paris. In Germany, he founded a short-lived periodical devoted to *musar* concepts; he also established many programs of adult education geared specifically for assimilated Jews. In Lithuania, he organized in 1877 an institute of advanced studies, designed to train Jewish educators according to his unique principles concerning inner growth. Based in Kovno, this seminary played an important role in the worldwide dissemination of *musar* ideas and practices.

Rabbi Salanter's skills as an organizer and administrator ensured that his movement would survive his death. He inspired several gifted disciples, each of whom strove in his own way to carry out Rabbi Salanter's vision of a revitalized and yet traditionally based Judaism. Perhaps inevitably, as the *musar* system increased in influence through the late nineteenth century, it experienced a gradual decline in its original freshness and intensity. For example, some of Rabbi Salanter's bold and innovative techniques of character development became overly institutionalized and were then rendered mechanical in various *yeshivot* throughout Eastern Europe. There were even student protests against *musar*; and, eventually, compromised and simplified versions of the basic teachings were accepted into many formal religious schools.

The specific precepts that Rabbi Salanter articulated will be explored in detail in the next chapter. Suffice it to say here, however, that he felt inner development involves much patience and lifelong devotion. He taught that the reason so few of us ever attain our inherent possibilities for accomplishment in the world is not due to our lack of good intentions, but to the weakness of our will. He never ceased to argue that our lower impulses are quite strong. Unless we actively enlist what he called specific ''strategems'' to conquer and transform these tendencies, he stressed, little real growth can occur. Judging from the ephemeral nature of most of our ''New Year's resolutions'' in our society, it is certainly clear what Rabbi Salanter had in mind.

The *musar* founder did, in fact, prescribe and introduce to various talmudic academies explicit methods for enhancing individual spiritual advancement. He stressed daily reading and meditation upon specific moralistic and inspirational texts, such as those by Rabbi Moses Chaim Luzzatto, an Italian poet and mystic of the eighteenth century. Rabbi Salanter also advocated techniques making use of dyads and groups—similar to modern group therapy—for he believed that we tend to avoid facing our true shortcomings. He also recommended that each person keep a daily journal or log to record progress in goal attainment. In a sense, he was an early behaviorist thinker, for he often wrote that we are creatures of habit—and strongly influenced by our environment.

Some of Rabbi Salanter's disciples went even further in devising strategems to combat the effects of habit on daily personality. For example, they would require the *yeshiva* student to enter a pharmacy and ask the proprietor for an absurd item, such as nails; or to board a train and then inform the attendant that he was without money; or to wear rags while mingling with well-dressed people. Such ego-effacing ''trials,'' of course, had long been part of Judaism and other time-honored spiritual traditions; *musar* aimed at inventing modern and effective versions of these.

Rabbi Salanter emphasized that without vigorous activities to strengthen our higher motivations, we are rarely able to actualize our latent potentials. "It is more difficult to change a single character trait than to learn the entire Talmud," he pointedly observed. On another occasion he similarly commented that, "It is more of a miracle to make a person into a *mensch* than it is to create a *golem* [a legendary being of clay]."

Interestingly, despite Rabbi Salanter's strong focus on the practical, day-to-day features of personal growth, he was no foe of mystical inquiry. True enough, he did not present formal lessons on the Kabbalah to his many students; nor did he advocate esoteric studies for those who lacked basic familiarity with more normative elements of Judaism. Yet, Rabbi Salanter insisted on the legitimacy of mystical practice for modern Jews—and the historical evidence suggests that his closest disciples were well acquainted with this exotic realm. Indeed, the founder of the *musar* movement viewed *Ruach Ha-Kadosh* (the Holy Spirit) as within the attainment of all; from this divine Source, he taught, emerge such qualities within us as extraordinary wisdom, discernment, and prophecy.

Rabbi Salanter stressed, however, that the patient, everyday, and seemingly mundane matter of emotional self-mastery is far more germane for most of us. He saw no shortcuts in the path toward complete character development—and no inner achievement without sustained effort and discipline. Perhaps his greatest legacy to us lies in his conviction that true moral perfection is possible, even in this industrial and secular age.

As this illustrious Jewish thinker and leader observed, "Man lives with himself for seventy years, but does not get to know himself." Today, as never before in modern times, men and women are eager for precisely such self-knowledge. It is to this intriguing realm that we now turn.

# The Universe Within

# FROM EARTH TO HEAVEN

Today we are in the midst of an exciting transformation in our approach to our inner world. The reductionist and mechanistic view that has long dominated Western thought is rapidly giving way to a more comprehensive outlook. Thus it no longer seems very convincing that we can gain important truths about human personality by studying lower species of animals. Nor does the notion that we are little more than complex neurological machines appear very tenable in the light of the considerable evidence that links our emotional and bodily well-being. Alongside such scientific conclusions, therapeutic practioners have begun to argue persuasively that we all possess a spectrum of attributes—ranging from primitive drives for physical survival to lofty capacities for creative and moral achievement.

At the same time, we are witnessing a dramatic shift in emphasis in psychology and related disciplines, from merely attempting to remove symptoms of emotional distress to enhancing our full potential within. A growing number of men and women have therefore begun to actively seek a new model to understand our personal makeup—a perspective to encompass the heights of what it means to be human. In this context, the realm of the sacred, the ecstatic, and the transcendent has once more become quite significant to many people.

As part of this new movement, there has been a tremendous resurgence of interest in humanity's great spiritual traditions—and their intriguing notions about our universe inside. For such traditions are proving far from archaic or outmoded; their longstanding teachings concerning human existence and the means to elevate ourselves seem as relevant in our all-night cities as in far distant eras and regions of the globe. It is becoming increasingly apparent that our mental characteristics have changed as little over the centuries as have our external features. This fact, no doubt, is an important factor in the growing allure that these systems of knowledge have for us in the technological age.

Judaism, however, has received scant attention from those sharing in the planetary rapprochement between science and spirituality. While other Western and many Eastern spiritual disciplines have been the subject of intensive study for their age-old wisdom, Jewish contributions to this vital realm have gone almost completely unexamined in modern times. This situation is quite ironic historically; for, as we have already seen, Judaism has for thousands of years been been intimately involved with individual self-growth. From the hills of Jerusalem to the villages of Eastern Europe, its sages have addressed this subject in considerable detail.

To be sure, it is no easy matter to penetrate some of the imposing veils that surround enduring Jewish thought on this topic. For instance, the technical terms that appear in many of the sacred texts are often far from accessible to the conceptual language of the twentieth century. This state of affairs is especially true for kabbalistic and Hasidic treatises, which are often multi-tiered with wordplay and symbolic meaning. The legends of the *Aggadah* and Midrash also do not initially seem particularly relevant to present concerns. Nor are classic Jewish themes about human personality and its higher reaches localized to a few well-defined sources; they are scattered throughout many disparate volumes. As we have noted earlier, the Talmud—the second most authoritative work in Judaism next to the Bible—is itself filled with diverging viewpoints on major issues.

Nevertheless, the task of describing the traditional Jewish outlook with regard to our inner world is far from impossible; precise allusions to our traits and capacities abound in the writings. Although such references are dispersed far and wide—across continents and epochs of the Diaspora—diligent research can bring them together into an organized whole. Also, several key Jewish thinkers have devoted themselves to the issue of self-improvement. Rather than simply offering a few aphorisms or parables on this important subject, they have accented it as central to their message for all Jews. In particular, three figures stand out historically for their lucid and inspiring work pertaining to inner development: Maimonides (1135–1204), Rabbi Moses Chaim Luzzatto (1707–1746), and Rabbi Israel Salanter (1810–1883).

Interestingly, each achieved renown for professional activity in a field besides Jewish scholarship—Maimonides as a physician, Rabbi Luzzatto as a poet, and Rabbi Salanter as an educator. And, each one suffered bitter criticism from more conventional-minded colleagues for articulating innovative ideas about our higher capabilities. The consensus of Jewish history, though, has elevated these three personages to lofty status indeed.

In this chapter and the two that follow, we will explore some of the chief Jewish principles related to personal growth; special attention will be accorded to the observations of these thinkers. In this manner, we will have the intellectual context to benefit more fully from the spiritual exercises presented in the third portion of this book. Due to the vastness of the subject matter, our focus will necessarily be narrowed to a few crucial concerns: namely, the metaphysical backdrop for our earthly existence, the nature of human personality, the essence of self-transformation, and the way to accentuate this process.

Judaism's traditional and poetic symbol for this entire topic is Jacob's vision of the celestial ladder. To climb its rungs with joy and balance is deemed our central purpose. For, as the Hasidic master Rabbi Nachman of Bratslav observed, the very path of self-knowledge leads us toward divine awareness. "Man is a miniature world," he declared. "If you learn to understand yourself . . . you can accomplish anything."

## Mission on Earth

It has been axiomatic in traditional Judaism that each person inhabits a universe filled with purpose and meaning. The Bible itself—especially the later Prophets—emphasizes the notion of individual responsibility and inner attainment. Such prophets as Isaiah, Joel, and Daniel affirm that our personal existence is essential to the divine plan—and that worthy men and women are capable of achieving *Ruach Ha-Kadosh* through their lofty daily conduct. Indeed, the ultimate enlightment of all humanity is promised in the prophecy of Joel, who said in God's name, "I will pour out My spirit on all flesh, [and] your sons and daughters shall prophesy (Joel 2:28)."

After the calamitous destruction of the Second Temple of Jerusalem, the early sages stressed the concept of individual growth. With the dissolution of the priesthood and all Temple observances, they taught that the meeting place between heaven and earth had moved to the heart of each person. Thus *Pirkey Avoth* clearly relates that, "Upon three things is the world based: upon the Law, upon service, and upon the practice of charity." Though most of the aphorisms in this sacred work reflect practical, everyday concerns, metaphysical references are also incorporated; these provide a definite perspective on the human condition.

In essence, the sages viewed every human life as holy and precious to the deity. The purpose of earthly existence, they explained, is to joyfully follow the moral code from on high. "Know from where you have come, where you are going, and before Whom you will in the future render account and reckoning," advises *Pirkey Avoth*. Through many other aphorisms, it accentuates that our deeds are all recorded and eventually judged. While the sages extolled the sanctity of earthly life, they also intimated quite definitely that we possess an immortal soul. "This world is like a vestibule to the World-to-Come," we are advised, "prepare yourself that you may enter into the banqueting hall."

While the early rabbis devoted little mention to the nature of the afterlife, they emphasized that each person has free choice to behave in a righteous manner. Two inclinations—the *yezer hara* and the *yezer tov* (usually translated loosely as "the evil inclination" and the "good inclination") are seen to challenge us in everyday existence; our response to these forces is what determines our station in the World to Come.

Several centuries later, the appearance of mystical works such as the *Bahir* and the *Zohar* added an intriguing dimension to traditional Jewish metaphysics. These provocative texts asserted that each person actually undergoes several lifetimes on earth—to be given the opportunity for complete self-development. Such esoteric writings portrayed human existence as a personal journey toward the divine—and stressed that daily life is the foundation for all higher evolution of the soul. For example, the thirteenth-century *Zohar* commented that, "The Holy One . . . permits [one] to start anew, and labor for himself in order to make good his deficiency . . . the man has to undergo transmigration because he is not . . . of great merit, since if he were so, he would not have to pass into another form and live again upon the earth, but would have at once 'a place better than sons and daughters.' "

It was Rabbi Isaac Luria, of sixteenth-century Safed, who dramatically infused Judaism with exciting metaphysical teachings about personal growth. In his powerful and superbly articulated vision, each of us here on earth is entrusted with a unique and specific "mission" to carry out for the Almighty. Rabbi Luria expounded that fallen sparks of the divine permeate all things in the universe; every individual has a definite sphere of influence for raising up these shards to their original Source—in a process he called *tikkun*, rectification. When the person succeeds in elevating all that he or she is meant to encounter, then it is time to advance upward to higher realms of existence.

Though Rabbi Luria did not write down any of his ideas, several of his closest disciples promulgated his message in their own writings; they also transmitted orally much of his elaborate system of thought. In the seventeenth and early eighteenth centuries, a variety of commentaries on the Lurianic Kabbalah were thereby circulated throughout Europe and the Near East. While many gifted thinkers sought to elucidate these evocative conceptions about individual achievement, few were as lucid or influential as Rabbi Moses Chaim Luzzatto. As a young Italian mystic, he was excommunicated by the rabbinical council of his region; its members were alarmed by his efforts to teach esoteric meditative techniques to ordinary folk. But Rabbi Luzzatto found refuge in Holland and there continued his brilliant discourses on the kabbalistic view of earthly life.

In such inspiring works as *The Way of God*, Rabbi Luzzatto provided a detailed exposition of our purpose as individuals dwelling in the material world. With extraordinary clarity and conciseness, he also addressed the perplexing issue of "why bad things happen to good people." In emphasizing the uniqueness of each person's existence, he stressed that we all have different tasks or *tikkunim* to accomplish.

"Every individual . . . has his own challenges . . . his assignment and responsibility in this world," Rabbi Luzzatto declared. "His deeds are then judged by God's attribute of justice with true precision, depending on the particular responsibility that was given to him.'' Rabbi Luzzatto further intimated that our problems in life should be understood as situations given us from above to prompt and spur our inner growth. ''According to this basic principle,'' he contended, ''all the gratifications and sufferings of this world exist as a challenge for man. The nature of each particular challenge is what the Highest Wisdom determines to be best for each particular individual.''

Not long after Rabbi Luzzatto's influential career, the Hasidic movement swiftly arose in Eastern Europe. Its charismatic founder, the Baal Shem Tov, took many of these compelling notions and cast them in the form of colorful parables and tales for the poor and uneducated Jewish masses. Central to his message was the concept that every person—no matter how seemingly lowly—has a unique mission on earth, ''a task that belongs to no other.'' Through many uplifting aphorisms recorded by his disciples, the Besht advised that we must each fully recognize and then energetically strive to fulfill our personal task. To do so will bring us true happiness and contentment, he observed. Thus the Baal Shem Tov preached that, ''The best way to the divine is the one to which your heart is drawn. Labor in it with your whole strength.'' On another occasion, he commented that, ''The Almighty has sent you into this world on an appointed errand. It is His will that you accomplish your errand in a state of joy.''

This perspective helped to form the metaphysical backdrop for the entire Hasidic milieu. In their far-reaching counseling, the early *rebbes* accented the view that we all have a unique purpose on the planet—and a unique set of inner qualities. As Rabbi Nachman of Bratslav, great-grandson of the Baal Shem Tov, poetically stated, ''God does not do the same thing twice.''

### The Two Inclinations

What precisely do the terms *yezer hara* and *yezer tov* connote? In the rabbinic literature, far more attention has been accorded to the *yezer hara* than to its seemingly more positive counterpart. Generally, the sages have seen the *yezer hara* to encompass our most selfish, destructive, and violent urges—those that represent, by their very nature, the lowest and most debased features of the human personality. In its more subtle or refined form, the *yezer hara* is viewed as comprising our petty desires for fame, power, and self-gratification at the expense of others.

## The Yezer Hara

Many statements in the talmudic and midrashic tradition add to the picture of the *yezer hara* as an evil, scheming "enemy" of all proper conduct. For example, one well-known aphorism in the Talmud asserts, "The *yezer hara* is problemsome in that [even] man's [basic] nature is called evil, as it is written, 'for the nature of man's heart is evil from his youth.'" Another talmudic comment pessimistically informs us that,

The *yezer tov* is poor and weak and has nothing to show as a reward for obedience to it. The *yezer hara* is strong. Whatever the former is able to acquire through tireless labor, the latter snatches away by holding forth the immediate reward of worldly pleasure.

Having personally witnessed—often through pain and torture— the depravity to which human behavior can sink, the sages were certainly realists to know the power of our darker impulses. Many early rabbis simply associated the *yezer hara*, therefore, with our capacity to act in antisocial and harmful ways. However, an alternate view has also existed for hundreds of years. Some Jewish thinkers have instead stressed the seemingly paradoxical talmudic dictum that, "The greater the man, the greater his *yezer hara*."

An *aggadic* story that sets forth this unusual concept is told about no less a dignitary than Abaye (278–338 C.E.), leader of the vibrant talmudic academy in Pumpedita, Babylonia.

He heard a certain man saying to a woman, "Let us arise betimes and go on our way." "I will," said Abaye, "follow them in order to keep them away from transgression," and he followed them for three parsangs across the meadows. When they parted company, he heard them say, "Our company is pleasant, the way is long." "If it were I," said Abaye, "I could not have restrained myself," and so went and leaned in deep anguish against a doorpost, when a certain old man came up to him and taught him: The greater the man, the greater his *yezer hara*.

As this vivid narrative implies, the term *yezer hara* may consequently be seen more accurately to represent our "passions"—a neutral force of bodily energy. Presumably, the more enlightened the individual, the more energy he or she has available for all forms of activity, lofty or otherwise. Indeed, Maimonides emphasized this interpretation of the *yezer hara* in his own writings and quoted the relevant talmudic maxim with approval.

In this context, Maimonides was undoubtedly aware of the classic Midrashic explanation of the words of Genesis, "And behold, it was very good!" The Midrash comments that the *yezer hara* is "to be considered very good . . . for without [it], man would not marry, build a house, beget children, or engage in business." From this obviously more favorable, or at least tolerant, portrayal of the *yezer hara*, it is actually a necessary attribute of our existence in the material world. With only our exalted impulses, the sages intimate, we would not be able to survive at all—either as a species or as individuals.

In the eighteenth century, the Hasidic founders strongly advanced this particular connotation of the *yezer hara*. To a populace uneducated and poor, they deemed our "passions" as potentially quite socially productive and capable of leading us to the realm of the divine. For example, the Baal Shem Tov expounded on the aphorism from *Pirkey Avoth*—"Who is powerful? He who subdues his *yezer hara*"—by advising his followers, "You should subdue your *yezer hara*, not kill it." In a similar vein, Rabbi Pinchas of Koretz remarked that, "Without the *yezer hara*, man could do no evil, but neither could he do good." In his view, its very presence gives us the moral choice to behave in beneficial ways.

Rabbi Israel Salanter, leader of the nineteenth-century *musar* movement, offered a slightly different perspective on this entire issue. In a variety of complex writings, he argued that the *yezer hara* is definitely a destructive force in our lives, but insisted that we can gain mastery over this part of ourselves through proper effort. Rabbi Salanter contended that two methods exist for accomplishing this challenging task: subjugation and transmutation. The former involves sheer repetition of many separate acts of self-denial—for example, feeling the desire to hurt someone emotionally, but consciously and repeatedly holding oneself back from doing so. The latter involves "impassioned thought and speech" coupled with habit—for instance, intense meditation on self-detachment as an alternative to vengeful anger, discussing the concept with a friend, and then practicing it each day.

Interestingly, Rabbi Salanter recommended subjugation of the *yezer hara* as a technique more suitable for middle-aged and older people. Conversely, he advocated transmutation as more appropriate for the young. His reasoning was that young people find it more difficult to suppress their desires and can more easily substitute new habits to replace the old. However, he asserted that transmutation is possible even for quite elderly persons, provided they are truly motivated to institute real changes in their habitual conduct.

It is important to note that major Jewish thinkers have never specifically associated the *yezer hara* with inborn or biological drives. The Talmud itself offers differing estimations as to when the *yezer hara* becomes potent in our development; the consensus seems to be that by the middle years of childhood, boys and girls possess the possibility for genuinely antisocial behavior as well as for emphatic, altruistic actions. The bar mitzvah and bat mitzvah ceremonies in part mark the youngster's clear attainment of the chronological capacity to recognize the difference between the two realms. Nevertheless, some longstanding Jewish sources seem to suggest that the *yezer hara* is intrinsic to our personality makeup as humans, and is therefore, in a sense, innate.

Ultimately, the exact nature of the *yezer hara* has remained somewhat elusive throughout the Jewish tradition. Perhaps this historical situation simply reflects the incomprehensibility of our propensities for malice and cruelty—qualities, after all, that no other animal species in the world exhibits. Certainly, modern researchers have come to no more conclusive answers on this troubling subject; for a while, Sigmund Freud's dark theory of a "death instinct" was well regarded, but it is generally discredited today. Nor have other twentieth-century theories demonstrated convincing validity. As the enigma of our inner depths continues to challenge us, we might best depart from this topic by calling to mind an appropriately mysterious passage from the Talmud.

In the Messianic Age, according to rabbinic teaching, God will destroy the *yezer hara* before the eyes of both the righteous and the wicked:

To the righteous, it will have the appearance of a tall mountain, and to the wicked it will have the appearance of a hair thread. But the former and the latter will weep. The righteous will weep, saying, "How were we able to overcome such a tall mountain!" The wicked will also weep, saying, "How is it that we were unable to conquer this hair thread!"

## *The* Yezer Tov

The other major force seen to operate within us is the *yezer tov,* usually translated as the "good inclination." Historically, the Jewish sages have devoted comparatively little explicit commentary to this human characteristic. In general, they have viewed the *yezer tov* as incorporating the impulses unique to our species in the most positive sense—such as our desires for justice, mercy, altruism, compassion, esthetics, creativity, and closeness to the divine.

The Jewish tradition is quite clear that these traits are not full-blown or even active during our early years of life, but rather must be cultivated deliberately. For instance, Maimonides observed that at birth we possess only the potential for such qualities, though any individual may have an inborn predisposition toward a particular one. "It is possible to be naturally disposed toward a virtue or a vice," he commented, "so that it is easier to perform the actions that accord with it." In this vein, we all have seen small children who, almost from their first steps, display a strong sense of fairness or empathy—and others who seem compelled by the need for self-expression in, say, art or music. In general, though, Maimonides reflected, "It is not possible for a man to possess virtue or vice by nature, from the beginning of his life, just as it is not possible for a man to possess one of the practical arts by nature."

Beginning in the kabbalistic era, Jewish sources increasingly articulate the notion that each of us comprises three distinct but interrrelated aspects to our being. These "levels of the soul" are known as the *nefesh, ruach,* and *neshamah* respectively—with two yet higher manifestations, *chayah* and *yechidah*, associated with the *neshamah*. In brief, the *nefesh* is said to contain our most primitive impulses for sheer survival. The *ruach* is seen as a more subtle bio-energy that sustains our physical well-being; like the *nefesh*, it is tied to the realm of the body, and dissipates with its demise.

The loftiest portion of the earthly Self is the *neshamah*; it is posited to be transcendent of time and space, and to be immortal. However, the *neshamah* is to some extent affected by its physical surroundings. *Chayah* and *yechidah* lie completely beyond material existence and are therefore unrelated to it; they are regarded as qualities of our Higher Self and become activated in loftier planes.

According to Jewish mystics, these varied components of the soul are all interconnected. In Rabbi Luzzatto's poetic simile, they are bound together like links in a chain. "Just as all these links comprise a single chain," he stated, "so do all the levels of the soul constitute a single entity, which is called the divine soul. . . . Each of these levels is bound to the one below it, until the lowest one is bound to the animal soul, which in turn is linked to the blood [and the body]."

The kabbalists further relate that the *neshamah* includes many different attributes by which we can attain perceptions of the divine. But they have emphasized that we must initiate conscious effort to awaken the *neshamah* from its dormant state in most of us. For example, the *Zohar* makes frequent reference to the radiant visions we can achieve, if we succeed in elevating our inner faculties. The *Zohar* explains,

These are three grades indissolubly united. If a man does well with his soul (*nefesh*), there descends upon him a certain crown called spirit (*ruach*), which stirs him to a deeper contemplation of the laws of the Holy King. If he does well with this spirit, he is invested with a noble, holy crown called super-soul (*neshamah*), which can contemplate all.

### *Kavvanah* and Imagination

For hundreds of years, major Jewish thinkers have emphasized the importance of two special attributes for our self-development. Both are considered part of the *neshamah* and crucial means to lead us to exalted realms of awareness; both are understood to be rather weak within most people and require regular and sustained practice to become dominant. In this respect, we would certainly not expect children or adolescents to have acquired them very significantly. These traits are known as *kavvanah* and higher imagination; we will examine each briefly in turn.

### Kavvanah: *Directed Consciousness*

The term *kavvanah* dates back to quite early sources in Judaism. In modern times, it has usually been mistranslated as simply either "concentration" or "feeling." However, if we analyze the origin of the word *kavvanah*, we immediately see that it derives from the

Hebrew root *kaven*, which means "to aim." Consequently, *kavvanah* more accurately denotes aiming our consciousness toward a specific goal, and hence the most apt translation is "directed consciousness."

In the oldest Jewish texts available, the sages stressed the need for *kavvanah* specifically during prayer and the performance of sacred acts. For example, they interpreted the biblical verse, "Hannah was speaking in her heart" (1 Samuel 1:13) to teach that "he who prays must direct his heart to heaven." In a like manner, Rabbi Bachya Ibn Paquda, an influential ethical writer of the eleventh century, commented in his famous *Duties of the Heart*, "When a man is employed in those duties in which both the heart and the limbs are involved—such as prayer—he should empty himself of all matter appertaining to this world or the next, and he should empty his heart of every distracting thought."

Several decades later, Maimonides offered similar instructions to spiritual seekers. He viewed this inner trait as essential for wholly experiencing sacred matters. Thus, in his *Code of Law*, he cogently stated, "What is the definition of *kavvanah*? It means that one should empty one's mind of all thoughts and see oneself as if one were standing before the Divine Presence." Later, in Maimonides's most important philosophical treatise, *The Guide for the Perplexed*, he similarly advised that *kavvanah* can be achieved through first banishing from awareness all worldly concerns and then focusing on the presence of the Holy One.

In the kabbalistic and later Hasidic tradition, *kavvanah* came to take on a much broader meaning—associated with our "will" or "intentionality." Mystical adepts regarded *kavvanah* as a state of higher consciousness, in which tremendous "one-pointed" concentration upon the divine is accomplished. Rather than seeing this quality as merely a necessary feature of formal prayer or religious conduct, they considered *kavvanah* to be the essence of transcendent experience. Though kabbalists have practiced many different methods of meditation to reach this goal—ranging from the ancient *Merkabah* system to intense concentration on the letters of the Hebrew alphabet, their common aim has been to develop their *kavvanah* to a state of true strength. For instance, the thirteenth-century *Zohar*, the bible of Jewish mysticism, clearly states that, "It is necessary to concentrate heart and mind on the letters."

In the eighteenth century, the Hasidic founders attached great importance to the cultivation of this quality. However, to their largely unlearned and impoverished followers, they contended that *kavvanah* can be developed in virtually any daily activity; it does not depend on elaborate or arcane meditative techniques. Indeed, the Baal Shem Tov's central message was that the myriad facets of everyday life are all avenues toward divine and ecstatic experience. They taught that whenever we devote ourselves fully—with absolute concentration and attentiveness—to any task that benefits others, we are strengthening our *kavvanah*. Thus if we go about the job of washing dishes with the right quality of mind, we are definitely enhancing our powers within.

The Hasidic leaders also emphasized that *kavvanah* involves learning to savor the present moment as an encounter with the Divine Presence in our lives. Rabbi Nachman of Bratslav particularly highlighted this aspect of "directed consciousness." Poetically, he observed that, "Man's world consists of nothing except the day and the hour that he stands in now. Tomorrow is a completely different world." On other occasion, he boldly stated that, "Yesterday and tomorrow do not exist."

The early Hasidic thinkers offered many parables and stories to illustrate the notion that our intentionality is vital to self-development. When our *kavvanah* is properly fortified, they explained, we possess a powerful ability to handle the vicissitudes of human existence. They viewed *kavvanah* as a means to inner harmony in everything we do.

There is a beautiful Hasidic tale that expresses this conviction: One day an acrobat came to the town of Krasny. He announced that he would cross the river on a rope stretched from bank to bank. Rabbi Chaim Krasner, a disciple of the Baal Shem Tov, stood by and observed the dangerous performance. His friends, noticing his deep concentration, asked him what in the performance caused him such depth of interest.

"I was thinking of the acrobat's ability to submit his life to danger," the Hasidic leader replied after a pause. "You might think that he does so for the money which an admiring crowd will shower upon him. But this is not so, for he if he thought this, he would surely fall into the river. His entire thinking must be concentrated upon one idea only," Rabbi Krasner continued, "namely, to maintain his balance—to prevent his body from inclining a hair's breadth to one side. His safety depends on his determination to keep upright without thought of reward. In this fashion, we all should cross over the narrow cord of life.''

### Higher Imagination

For hundreds of years, Jewish thinkers have emphasized another key quality of the *neshamah* essential for higher consciousness: namely, that of imagination. Though today we generally denigrate this inner characteristic and associate it with idle fantasy or entertainment, the sages have long considered it the very gateway to divine awareness. They have viewed its proper development as crucial to self-improvement and prescribed many methods for its awakening. It would be no exaggeration to say that, without an elevated imagination, we are deemed only partially in control of our full capabilities.

Maimonides has probably articulated the relevance of imagination for self-growth more precisely than any other major teacher in Judaism. In such influential works as *The Guide for the Perplexed*, he set forth specific principles which have served as the foundation for considerable commentary and practice ever since. Consistent with his overall approach to our inner life, he contended that imagination is a trait that operates in both a coherent and comprehensive manner. If we understand its nature and how to use it appropriately, Maimonides insisted, we can even attain the realm of prophecy—the loftiest state possible according to Jewish tradition.

In day-to-day activity, Maimonides asserted, our imagination acts in a rather mundane way.

Part of the function of the imaginative faculty is . . . to retain sensory impressions, to combine them, and chiefly to form images. [However] . . . the principal and highest function is performed when the senses are at rest in their action, for then it receives, to some extent, divine inspiration . . . this is the nature of dreams which prove true and also of prophecy.

Maimonides further related that the more enlightened we become, the greater the strength of our imagination and our capacity for transcendent experience. In the ordinary person, this trait is fairly weak and tied closely to lower needs; petty and fleeting bodily desires rule over it. Images of self-aggrandizement likewise dominate. As a result, the average individual is unable to make use of his or her image-making faculty for more exalted perceptions.

Certainly, modern research strongly confirms that most of us devote literally hours each waking day to trivial and anxious day-dreaming—a situation that has apparently changed little over the centuries. But if we strive to alter our habitual mindset, Maimonides insisted, "to suppress every thought or desire for unreal power and dominion . . . for victory, increase of followers, acquisition of honor"—we can achieve tremendous powers of creativity and insight.

Jewish mystics have traditionally found Maimonides's provocative ideas on imagination to be quite exciting. From the kabbalists' often visionary perspective, we all typically make poor use indeed of this potentially extraordinary attribute. They have therefore prescribed for many centuries specific techniques to direct our imagination toward higher spheres. The sacred letters of the Hebrew alphabet have been one major tool to accomplish this task. Some methods have also been based on biblical images and those of the *Zohar*, whose surrealist motifs have been prized for their mind-expanding qualities. In a somewhat less direct manner, the vivid and poetic tales of the Midrash have undoubtedly served this same purpose historically for the majority of Jews, unacquainted with the subtleties of the Kabbalah.

Underlying all such approaches has been the notion that imagination is a vital feature of our *neshamah*—and capable of bringing us to divine perceptions. As Rabbi Nachman of Bratslav aptly remarked, "Man has an image-making faculty, which is one of the most important forces in his life." In our own time, Rabbi Abraham Isaac Kook, Chief Rabbi of Palestine prior to the establishment of modern Israel, put the matter quite clearly. "The perception of ontological truth," he observed, "is dependent upon the development of the power of imagination, a special, non-rational faculty."

### The Gateway of Dreams

No discussion of traditional Jewish thought about human personality would be complete without mentioning the topic of dreams. For millennia, Judaism has recognized the importance of dreams as signposts for our lives. The Bible contains several major allusions to dreams; in the narratives concerning Joseph and Daniel, for example, dreams are seen to communicate divine messages. They are therefore depicted as imparting knowledge of events beyond the ordinary bounds of time and space. Since biblical days, the sages have generally highlighted the more practical value of dreams for enhancing our personal well-being. To fully elevate our inner makeup, they have taught, we must understand the nature of our dreams.

As far back as the talmudic era, Jewish sources have articulated a rather coherent approach to dreams. Scattered throughout the volumes of the Talmud are a variety of specific references to their significance; though nearly fifteen hundred years old, these ideas are quite up to date in their formulation. Together, they suggest that the sages viewed dreams as essentially reflections of waking consciousness, rather than as mysterious forces. They considered dreams worthy of serious attention for the light they could shed on a person's innermost thoughts. And, they seemed to regard repetitive dreams as especially noteworthy. "What we speak of by day, we dream of by night," and "A dream that is not interpreted is like a letter undeciphered" are two classic talmudic aphorisms on this subject.

Generally, the sages extolled our possibility for transcendent experience within dreams, but stressed their pragmatic aspects. Largely through implicit means—such as Midrashic legend—they intimated that the extraordinary dreams of Joseph and other lofty figures resulted from their enlightened state of mind and that more typical individuals are scarcely likely to receive such celestial messages. Interestingly, the Talmud anticipated the most contemporary critique of modern dream analysis in its notion that "The interpretation of a dream sometimes determines the actual event." Whether cynically intended or not, this remark seems to indicate that the early scholars recognized the inherent difficulties in making definitive statements about any particular dream.

Several centuries later, kabbalistic thinkers addressed in significant detail the subject of dreams. Reflecting their interest in our nonrational and intuitive capabilities, they raised dreams to a high place in their metaphysical system and meditative practice. For example, the *Zohar* is replete with many references to dreams. More than six hundred years before Freud startled the scientific world with his assertion that dreams convey vital meaning, this thirteenth-century mystical work outlined a thorough theory of dream analysis. To this day Jewish mystics base virtually their entire approach to dreams on the provocative ideas of the *Zohar*.

In brief, this esoteric text affirms the talmudic contention that dreams chiefly mirror our daily state of mind; it emphasizes that out ordinary waking consciousness greatly influences their characteristic content. Thus we are specifically informed that because King David waged war and bloodshed during his life, his dreams were likewise bloody and violent. More generally, the *Zohar* relates the fundamental principle that "God communicates to each man by means of dreams, by the degree and shade of color conformable to the degree and shade of color of the man himself." Or, more concisely, "No man is shown anything in a dream except what falls in his own grade."

Nevertheless, the *Zohar* advises that the greater our self-development, the more we become receptive to divine information in dreams. As we systematically strengthen our *neshamah*—especially our qualities of *kavvanah* and imagination—the heavenly gates will swing open. When our petty desires and worries no longer dominate our dreams, they are transformed into sacred vessels. Therefore, the *Zohar* comments, "To the righteous, no false messages are communicated [in a dream], but all they are told is true."

For this reason, kabbalists have long advocated that we strive to recall and interpret our dreams. Some of the most influential Jewish mystics have kept diaries or logs of their dreams, a practice consistent with the *Zohar*'s dictum that, "A dream that is not remembered might as well have not been dreamed." A comprehensive look at traditional Jewish dream analysis would take us beyond our scope; however, we might note that the key technique has been to interpret by certain rules dream symbols—personal and universal—as well as even colors and numbers. A similar approach, of course, was advanced by Freud in his landmark book *The Interpretation of Dreams*, published in 1900. Indeed, the fascinating parallels between psychoanalytic and kabbalistic dream analysis appear far from accidental, as several modern researchers have demonstrated.

In the Hasidic period, *rebbes* frequently made use of dream interpretation as part of their spiritual counseling. Many decades before Freud's bold forays into the hidden regions of the psyche, *rebbe* and Hasid together sifted through dream material to understand what it signified. Their goal was to determine the dream's meaning in terms of *hirhurey d'yoma*—the thoughts and desires of the day. To accomplish this, the *rebbe* sought to sort out the jumble of images and symbols in the Hasid's dream. These were described as emanations from the world of *tohu*, chaos, yet possessing their own logic and coherence.

For example, Rabbi Nachman of Bratslav respectfully observed of dreams, "[They] are rooted in a very sublime level, though man, for lack of proper development, may not recognize this." Emphasizing the age-old notion that dreams can offer us transcendent experiences, this brilliant visionary commented that, "Depending on how the imaginative facility is developed, dreams may be false and worthless or true and prophetic."

Through all their spiritual counseling, the Hasidic leaders stressed our capability for higher consciousness, whether in dreams or waking activity. But in keeping with centuries of traditional Jewish thought, they insisted that our intentionality determines the inner heights we attain. The divine may manifest in our lives, but we must consciously decide to meet it.

As the Hasidic master Rabbi Pinchas of Koretz poetically commented, "Man contains within himself all the worlds that exist. He is, therefore, able to have contact with them all. Man possesses within himself all good and evil traits, but they are in an unborn state; it is within his power to give them birth."

## 3

# CLIMBING THE CELESTIAL LADDER

It is crucial to realize that the Jewish sages have never embraced a static model of human personality. Fundamental to their teachings is the notion that we each have an inborn affinity to grow in emotional and spiritual strength. In one vivid simile, the Talmud comments that every person harbors potential good deeds within as a pomegranate contains seeds; our potentials for creativity and achievement are deemed almost limitless. For this reason, the Talmud advises, "Do not despise an ignorant man who strives to gain knowledge, or a man of ill repute who strives to redeem his past."

Throughout Jewish history the time-honored symbol for personal growth has been Jacob's ladder. Not only has this evocative image inspired artists and poets down the centuries, but moralists and philosophers as well. Imaginative writers too have found the celestial ladder to be a powerful source of creative energy. Before we explore some of its unique significance for our own time, it might prove worthwhile to look at its actual biblical context.

In the account of Genesis (28:10–22), Jacob is pursued by his brother Esau, a fearsome warrior and debauched character. Jacob is aware that his very life is in danger as he prepares to sleep in the night wilderness. He assembles a pile of stones as his pillow.

"And he dreamed that there was a ladder set up on the earth," Genesis relates, "and the top of it reached to heaven. And behold, the angels of God were ascending and descending upon it! And behold, the LORD stood above it." God then appears to Jacob and reaffirms the divine covenant made to his father and grandfather, Isaac and Abraham. Upon awakening, Jacob consecrates the site using oil and vows to serve the Almighty. In homage, he also erects a pillar to make the site suitable for worship and then goes on his way. Interestingly, the Midrash recounts that this spot—which Jacob describes as the "gate of heaven"—was the future site of the Temple of Jerusalem, and consequently the most sacred place on earth.

Over millenia, many Jewish commentators have offered their interpretations on the symbolic importance of this narrative. They have consistently viewed the ladder in particular as both a vivid depiction of the human condition and a prescription for reaching the transcendent world. Kabbalists have specifically seen the ladder as radiant with subtle and sublime meanings for imparting a deeper understanding of the cosmos. Not surprisingly, Hasidic and *musar* leaders have often alluded in their public talks and writings to the celestial ladder; they have also valued it as an image for guided meditation. Indeed, the heavenly ladder has probably stood for the nature of individual advancement more centrally than any other symbol in Judaism.

But what does Jacob's starry vision say to us in the late twentieth century? Does it really have much relevance for our own needs and aspirations? It is a basic dictum of Jewish mystics that the sacred tradition speaks simultaneously on many levels—and to every person in every generation. Therefore, if this intriguing account in Genesis has inspired countless men and women around the globe for centuries, then it undoubtedly possesses the same archetypal power today. Later in this book you will be invited to meditate in a personal way upon the celestial ladder; but for now, let us briefly examine some of its longstanding significance.

### Health, Family, and Livelihood

For one thing, the ladder's base stands firmly upon the earth, which suggests that we need to be properly rooted or grounded as a prerequisite for all higher experience. The sages have always insisted that without a solid foundation in the everyday world, our ascent toward the divine is inevitably fraught with danger and indeed, doomed to certain collapse. It is no historical accident that even the most ardent Jewish mystics have emphasized the importance of mundane existence—with all its seeming trivialities—as the doorway leading to the most exalted realms of the deity. They have repeatedly stressed that unless we first master the practical aspects of daily living—such basics as our health, family relations, and livelihood—we cannot possibly hope to move on successfully to loftier spheres.

Consistent with talmudic precepts on this concept, Maimonides thus devoted extensive attention to delineating the role of proper diet, regular physical exercise, and attractive surroundings as means to strengthen our capacity for higher awareness. In a holistic outlook that antedates the most current notions in behavioral medicine and psychology, he insisted that our bodily, emotional, and spiritual qualities constitute an inviolate unity. Consequently, even in Maimonides's treatises on philosophy and ethics, he provided a variety of specific recommendations for achieving physical well-being and for healing illness.

"Preserving the body's health and vigor is among the ways of the Lord," Maimonides cogently observed, "for to attain understanding and knowledge is impossible when one is sick . . . a man needs to keep away from things that destroy the body and to accustom himself to things that make him healthy and vigorous."

In a similar manner, the Hasidic founders strongly emphasized the links that connect mind, body, and spirit. They advised their numerous followers that emotional problems often lead to health disorders—and pinpointed chronic anger and sadness as particularly harmful in their bodily effects. For instance, Rabbi Nachman of Bratslav commented that, "Melancholy oftentimes presages illness," and "He who is sad brings upon himself many afflictions." On another occasion, he pointedly remarked, "Happiness is the remedy for all kinds of diseases—because many illnesses are caused by depression." His message was quite in keeping with the Baal Shem Tov's original teaching that bodily vitality enables us to adopt a joyful and energetic approach to life. Indeed, the Besht was celebrated for his power as a healer and his knowledge of the body's hidden ways.

Jewish thinkers have also traditionally viewed day-to-day family and social life as another important base of the celestial ladder. In historical periods before ours, there was usually very little opportunity for individual independence or anonymity; virtually all men and women were inextricably involved in a lifetime network of familial and communal responsibilities. Consequently, some age-old spiritual systems have seen such duties at best as irrelevant to personal development; at worst, they have been condemned as ensnarements to be avoided as much as possible. Yet, Judaism has never venerated cloistered seclusion from others or monasticism as a way of life. "Do not separate yourself from the community" is a dictum that dates far back, to *Pirkey Avoth* in the third century C.E. Even the most celebrated Jewish mystics have been closely involved with the ongoing affairs of their communities—and they have characteristically been married with children.

In the kabbalistic and later Hasidic tradition, our marital and familial relationships have a higher significance indeed. They are regarded as reflecting very real ties to past lifetimes on earth and as essential to the cosmic process of *tikkun*, rectification. For hundreds of years, such exalted texts as the *Zohar* have related that each person's parents, spouse, children, friends, and other intimates are central to his or her own purpose on this plane of existence; for this reason, Jewish mystics have contended that there are no accidents or coincidences in our important relationships in life.

For example, the *Zohar* explains that marital partners are placed together on earth for a very special task in aiding redemption. "All spirits are composed of male and female, and when they go forth into the world, they go forth as both male and female, and afterwards, the two elements are separated," we are told. "If a man is worthy, they are afterwards united, and it is then that he truly meets his mate and there is a perfect union both in spirit and flesh."

In the sixteenth century, Rabbi Isaac Luria and his fellow mystics in Safed elevated this notion to a primary position in their vast metaphysical system. They expounded that through family relationships we are given the valuable opportunity to raise up the divine sparks that lie within all forms in the universe—including ourselves and those around us. With the proper *kavvanah* or intentionality, they taught, each of us can help bring about the primal Harmony; the way to the divine lies precisely through our everyday relationships.

The Hasidic leaders strongly emphasized this provocative notion in counseling individual men and women. Through a variety of therapeutic and inspirational techniques—ranging from dream interpretation and shock to storytelling and humor—they endeavored to help the Hasid see family life in a transformed manner.

Rather than accepting the complaining Hasid's definition of the situation—that, say, a parent or a spouse was guilty of intolerable arrogance or rudeness—the *rebbe* might extol the supposed offender as a marvelous spiritual teacher in disguise, assisting the Hasid in learning emotional control or egolessness in the crucible of daily routine.

This outlook on family dynamics was often quite effective, for both the *rebbe* and Hasid knew that Judaism had long incorporated such a perspective. After all, the Midrash was filled with legends of Elijah and his many guises to challenge and enlighten the complacent. Other classic tales in Jewish folklore, such as those about the *Lamed-vov*—the thirty-six hidden saints in every generation who sustain the world—likewise conveyed the idea that we usually learn our major lessons in life from seemingly ordinary people and unremarkable situations. Strongly influenced by this enduring view of things, nearly everyone could catch glimpses of the divine in the commonplace; the transcendent did not seem so far away.

In our own time, there are many benefits to be gained from adopting this traditional Jewish perspective. Certainly, it offers a much-needed counterbalance to the pervasive cynicism and gloom in our wider culture today. For instance, in a recent discussion on Jewish mysticism and its contemporary relevance, a lively middle-aged woman related to our group that she had been burning with resentment several years earlier in her life, for having to care for her elderly, senile mother. The situation had begun to deteriorate for her into an intolerable burden, so she had sought the advice of her personal *rebbe*—who was both a practicing psychotherapist and a teacher of the Kabbalah.

"Would you be pleased if you were suddenly presented with a wonderful spiritual teacher meant just for you?" her *rebbe* asked.

"Of course," the woman instantly replied, "I'd be more than pleased—I'd be overjoyed!"

"Well," her *rebbe* continued, "you have your wonderful spiritual teacher in your mother now. Go and learn from her."

The woman concluded this story by commenting that she immediately saw her whole, difficult relationship in a new light—and found that she possessed the strength to make her mother's last years rewarding for both of them.

In traditional Jewish thought, livelihood is considered a third necessary foundation in the ladder of self-improvement. An age-old

talmudic adage says, "He who does not teach his sons an occupation is as though he has taught them to steal." Judaism has always
revered the everyday world of work as an important field for improving our character. As noted in Chapter 1, the early sages who
lived after the destruction of the Second Temple of Jerusalem refused to create a special class of Torah scholars; they felt that such
a caste would constitute a violation of the divine command that all
persons are equal in their purpose on earth. Thus the sages warned
strongly against seeking material rewards for sacred study, and
declared that financial security should be obtained through some
other form of daily activity.

In keeping with this outlook, even the greatest sages had specific
trades by which they earned a living. Hillel was a carpenter, Joshua
ben Hananiah a smith, Johanan a shoemaker. Nearly a thousand
years later, Maimonides declined to receive any monetary compensation for his far-flung involvements on behalf of the Cairo Jewish
community and others that sought his assistance. In the Hasidic
era, the Baal Shem Tov, while still unrevealed to the world, supported himself for many years as a teacher's aide, then as a digger
of lime, and later as an innkeeper. Some of his most celebrated
disciples, who went on to establish important Hasidic groups, often
earned their livelihoods in similar circumstances.

The Hasidic leaders stressed the importance of work for two key
reasons. First, they viewed it as a superb way to strengthen the
quality of *kavvanah* or intentionality. To succeed in maintaining
a higher state of consciousness in the devotional atmosphere of
the House of Study was deemed little real training at all, but to
exercise inward "binding" to the deity in the bustle of the
marketplace—*that* was a true challenge. Rabbi Nachman of Bratslav
addressed this issue quite explicitly. He commented that,
"[In] . . . the time a person spends working . . . the goal is to sift
out the sparks of holiness and elevate them . . . . All the worlds
are [thereby] elevated and awesome *tikkunim* [rectifications] are
achieved."

The Hasidic founders also emphasized that work can help us
develop many of our other higher faculties. In innumerable ways,
we can acquire superior emotional and intellectual traits, they taught,
by taking the proper attitude to what we are doing. Such important
inner characteristics as decisiveness, clarity of thought, reliability,

orderliness, and self-discipline can all be learned from the necessity of earning a living, Rabbi Nachman declared,

No one is entitled to excuse his lack of service to the Lord by affirming that he is engaged in business and must associate with vulgar folk. God is everywhere. He is among the most common of men; He is to be found in the lowliest occupation. Delve deeper and you will a way to serve God in everything and in every work and place.

In fact, many colorful Hasidic tales point to the specific dangers that surround a person who is no longer obligated to maintain any livelihood; loss of purpose and then self-destruction are often seen to result. In our own era, of course, mounting evidence from many studies has convincingly shown that involvement in work is central to our mental and physical well-being—and that its sudden absence can be quite devastating, especially during later adulthood.

For a second major reason, the early Hasidic *rebbes* regarded work as vital to our self-development: It allows us an important means to express who we are as unique individuals. In this respect, the *rebbes* set forth strikingly up-to-date notions of ''career counseling,'' for they viewed livelihood as a way we can help fulfill our deepest talents, skills, and interests. Of course, there was little economic opportunity for Jews in the impoverished villages of Eastern Europe. Few people possessed the capital necessary to establish a successful business; skilled artisans were rare.

Nevertheless, while they recognized the limited economic sphere surrounding them, many Hasidic leaders sought to guide their followers to derive some personal fulfillment in whatever work they did for a living. At times, the *rebbes* imparted advice that took the form of recommending specific changes in occupation. These could be quite radical in nature; Hasidic tales attest to wealthy merchants who became secluded scholars, and scholars who became ritual slaughterers or even wagon drivers at their *rebbe*'s behest. In other instances, the *rebbe* recommended that the Hasid strive to find greater moral or creative challenges in life without shifting occupation.

In general, the compelling teachings of the Baal Shem Tov directed Hasidic thinking on this entire issue. Every individual is here on earth for a specific mission, he declared; our livelihood may be central to that divine task.

No two persons have the same abilities. Each man should work in the service of God according to his own talents. If one man tries to imitate another, he merely loses his opportunity to do good through his own merit, and he cannot accomplish anything by imitation of the other's service.

## Higher Consciousness

Throughout Jewish history, the symbol of Jacob's ladder has carried with it other significances. Though its base indeed stands solidly on earth, its pinnacle is seen to stretch into the very reaches of paradise. The major Jewish thinkers have always emphasized that we each have the capacity to achieve almost unimaginable heights of inner perfection. No gates are deemed barred to us, except those we shut on our own; there is an unbroken path from the everyday world to the supernal realms, they have taught. "Piety brings about humility," the Talmud explains, "humility brings about fear of sin; fear of sin brings about holiness; holiness brings about the holy spirit."

Several centuries later, Maimonides developed a comprehensive system of personal development designed to accomplish precisely such a process. He integrated biblical, talmudic, and Midrashic teachings to articulate a series of definite principles by which, he contended, any person could eventually attain the most exalted states of consciousness. It is significant that Maimonides viewed *Pirkey Avoth* as the foundation for all such endeavor. Though this classic work is outwardly not esoteric at all, but rather pragmatic in its advice, Maimonides plainly stated:

They [the sages], peace be upon them, said: "Whoever wants to become a pious man should fulfill the words of *Avoth*." According to us, there is no rank above piety except for prophecy, the one leading to the other. As they said, "Piety brings about the holy spirit." Thus, from what they have said, it is clear that following the discipline described in this tractate leads to prophecy.

Maimonides regarded the process of ascent to transcendent awareness as involving a gradual refinement of our mental nature. By carefully analyzing biblical and other references to the attributes of prophecy, he concluded that, in each person, the presence of character flaws acts as a "veil" or barrier to loftier experience. In general, the more emotional and intellectual flaws we have, the greater our separation from the divine world.

Know that no prophet prophesies until after he acquires all the rational [intellectual] and most of the moral [emotional] virtues, that is, the important ones. To possess the moral virtues in their entirety, to the extent of not being impaired by any vice at all, is not one of the conditions of prophecy . . . [but] some moral vices, such as irascibility, prevent prophecy entirely . . . . The same holds for anxiety and grief.

Thus this brilliant philosopher-physician contended that true self-development means the gradual elimination of our personality flaws—and the simultaneous strengthening of our higher impulses, stemming from the *yezer tov*. In this way, we can systematically remove the barriers that limit our climb upward. In keeping with previous Jewish thought on this subject, Maimonides depicted Moses as the paragon or exemplar of the spiritually evolved individual. "When our Moses knew that no veils remained which he had not pierced and that all the moral virtues and all the rational virtues had become perfected in him, [then] he sought to perceive the true reality of God's existence, since no obstacle was left."

Maimonides's systematic presentation of principles for self-improvement inspired generations of spiritual seekers. His writings soon aroused considerable excitement among mystics as well as ethical thinkers, who intuitively shared his inherent optimism in our great possibilities for achievement in life. They shared his strong conviction that we possess tremendous, unused resources within. However, advocates for this viewpoint have not always been well received by their more conservative peers; through the centuries, the rabbinical establishment has been very wary of such doctrines because of their potentially heretical implications.

For example, in the late thirteenth century, Abraham Abulafia experienced severe censure for his promulgation of mind-expanding techniques based on the letters of the Hebrew alphabet. Though his methods have become revered as lustrous gates to the divine, he was condemned in his own lifetime as a threat to mainstream Judaism. Rabbi Moses Chaim Luzzatto was excommunicated in eighteenth-century Italy for similarly offering specific teachings—partly derived from Maimonides's work—on how to achieve the prophetic state of consciousness.

In such provocative books as *The Way of God* and *The Path of the Just*, Rabbi Luzzatto articulated the notion that we can all learn to attain *Ruach Ha-Kadosh* through proper preparation. He stressed that significant effort is necessary to accomplish that end, but denied that it is an overwhelmingly difficult task.

Prophecy therefore requires a course of apprenticeship just as in the case of other disciplines and crafts, where one must advance step by step until he masters them thoroughly. This explains what the Bible means when it speaks of the "sons of the prophets." These were the ones who apprenticed themselves to recognized prophets in order to learn the necessary ways of prophecy.

In fact, while still a young man and unmarried, Rabbi Luzzatto claimed to have experienced visions of Elijah and other ascended masters. Though Rabbi Luzzatto initially outraged his rabbinical colleagues with such pronouncements, he became revered after his death among Jews all over Europe and the Near East. His lucid writings inspired many people with his quiet confidence in our latent potential.

Those who train themselves for prophecy must do so through a number of specific disciplines. The purpose of these is to bring the Highest Influence to bear on them and nullify the effects of their physical nature holding it back. In this manner, they attach themselves to God, and bring upon themselves a revelation of His Light.

In a similar manner, the Hasidic founders extolled our capacities for self-advancement. In general, they argued that while we typically go through our days in a state of only dim awareness, we are each capable of the highest experiences of the divine. In simple teachings to the unlearned, they relied upon parables and stories to emphasize that self-reflection, discipline, and strong devotion (*devekuth*) to the Holy One, can enable any person to attain lofty inner realms. To a people who felt powerless and demoralized, the early *rebbes* affirmed the talmudic maxim that, "All beginnings are difficult." But the crucial matter, they insisted, is to tread firmly each step until the ladder's heights are scaled.

"An action is not an action until it is carried through from the realm of possibility to that of actuality," Rabbi Nachman of Bratslav observed. His colleague Rabbi Yerachmiel of Parischa likewise encouraged his followers, "Begin in a modest way, maintain an honest effort to attain higher and higher realms and . . . you shall attain undreamed of heights of perception."

Indeed, in the Hasidic outlook, individuals like the Baal Shem

Tov and his closest disciples had truly achieved superhuman status through their devoted and joyful efforts to reach the transcendent world. Countless Hasidic tales celebrate the remarkable powers of the *zaddik*—even being able to penetrate the veils of space, time, and energy, to accomplish necessary *tikkunim* or vital acts of redemption. In their most exalted levels of functioning, Hasidic stories relate, the Besht and his associates could ascend to the halls of paradise, meet with angels and righteous departed souls, and intervene in their doings to help men and women on earth; if deemed necessary, they would not hesitate to challenge the very deliberations of the Heavenly Tribunal in order to achieve a merciful judgment for those still struggling toward self-perfection.

This notion represents yet another facet of Jacob's ladder and its relevance for our inner growth. Historically, Judaism has always considered quite significant the description from Genesis that the angels Jacob beheld were "ascending and descending" upon the celestial ladder. For hundreds of years, Jewish sages have interpreted this account to signify that visionary experience is by itself only a partial fulfillment of the divine plan; we must actively make use of such perception to assist others. For this reason, the Jewish tradition has never embraced the motif of the detached or removed spiritual master, perhaps dispassionately sitting in a cave high up in the mountains. In fact, Hasidic legend asserts that the sole purpose for the Baal Shem Tov's personal existence on earth was that, in his previous lifetime, he had failed to share the "fragrance of his wisdom" with those around him.

The Jewish ideal has thus been for the truly self-perfected individual to remain concerned and involved with others. The sixteenth-century mystic Solomon Alkabez referred to such souls as "those who return [to earthly life] not on account of their having omitted a religious duty, let alone for having committed a trespass, but solely out of compassion with their contemporaries." Typically expressed more through folktales and myths than through philosophical discourse, this theme reverberates throughout traditional Judaism.

For instance, the Midrash relates that Elijah was entrusted with the sacred responsibility of aiding forlorn and needy individuals on this planet. Many stories recount how, disguised as a beggar or lowly laborer, he performed some key act of service to give renewed strength of heart or courage to one in despair. The colorful legends of the *Lamed-vov* likewise communicate this important teaching. Freed from the constraints of fame, these thirty-six righteous souls in every generation are seen to assist in sustaining and illuminating the world.

Interestingly, this feature of Jewish thought related to self-advancement has close parallels with aspects of other ancient spiritual systems. For example, Buddhism has long venerated the role of the Bodhisattva, the perfected master who voluntarily returns to earthly existence to selflessly uplift those still chained to the wheel of karma. In this way, we are all viewed as connected in destiny.

The evocative symbol of Jacob's ladder provides us with many important implications for our personal growth; meditation upon it inevitably leads to further insights on the nature of our relation to the divine. With the proper *kavvanah*, intentionality, we can truly gain the wisdom to comprehend the diverse subtleties inherent in this biblical passage and image. As Rabbi Mendel of Kotzk commented, ''Man contains within . . . all the worlds that exist . . . He possesses within . . . all good and evil traits, but they are in an unborn state; it is within his power to give them birth.''

From its base firmly planted on the earth to its pinnacle in paradise, the ladder stretches before the vista of our daily lives. It beckons for us now to ascend.

# 4

# HELPING THE ASCENT

O ver the many centuries, Jewish thinkers have not been content merely to advance a theoretical model about inner growth. Rather, they have actually provided concrete suggestions for how each of us can accentuate the process of self-development. Underlying virtually all traditional Jewish guidelines on this vital topic have been two fundamental notions: that our social environment exerts a tremendous effect upon us as individuals; and that habit is a powerful force, which can either help or hinder our ascent toward the divine.

### The Importance of Habit

Since the ancient days of the Mishnah, Jewish thought has emphasized that we are very much influenced by those around us. While the early sages cherished our capacities for wisdom and judgment, they recognized quite clearly that we can be easily misled by the wrong surroundings. Few of us have such a secure sense of self-identity as to be able to triumph repeatedly over opposing values, they taught.

True enough, *Pirkey Avoth* urges, "In a place where there are no [righteous] men, strive to be a [righteous] man." But, in a sense, to be in such a situation is hardly seen as ideal; this same inspiring work offers many aphorisms proclaiming the importance of being in a place where there are indeed others to emulate and learn from. *Pirkey Avoth* persistently stresses this necessity, as well as that of deliberately avoiding destructive or negative influences. It clearly implies the personal benefits we can experience in associating with proper mentors and specifies a variety of everyday situations—

apparently, just as common seventeen hundred years ago as today—that we should shun as much possible. These include gossip, malicious humor, and trivial conversations in general.

As the paragon of Jewish medieval rationalism, Maimonides strongly maintained the talmudic outlook on this issue. He argued throughout his diverse writings that we are extremely susceptible to environmental forces. Though this brilliant philosopher and physician possessed high regard for our latent potential, he was a realist and an astute psychological observer. Thus Maimonides commented in his *Laws Concerning Character Traits*,

Man is created in such a way that his character traits are influenced by his neighbors and friends, and he follows the customs of the people in his country. Therefore, a man needs to associate with the just and be with the wise continually, in order to learn [from] their actions, and to keep away from the wicked, who walk in darkness, so that he avoids learning from their actions.

Maimonides went even further in his estimation of the powerful impact—for both good or evil—that our surroundings have upon us. Highlighting the biblical maxim "Cleave to the wise and their disciples," he prescribed such specific activities as marrying into the families of the wise, eating and drinking with their disciples, doing business on behalf of their disciples, and "associating with them in all kinds of associations."

Conversely, Maimonides warned vehemently against inhabiting an area where unethical and mean-spirited people abound. Having been forced to lead an unhappy, nomadic life due to religious persecution, he no doubt spoke from heartfelt conviction when he vividly and almost poignantly declared,

If one is in a country with evil customs, where men do not follow the right way, he shall go to a place where men are just and they follow the way of good men. If all the countries he knows or hears about follow a way that is not good, as in our own time, or if . . . he is unable to go to a city with good customs, he shall dwell alone in solitude . . . [if necessary], he shall go off to the caves, the briers, or the desert, and not accustom himself to the [wrong] way.

In the early eighteenth century, Rabbi Moses Chaim Luzzatto similarly emphasized the importance of environmental influences on character development. As the most significant Jewish ethical writer in his era, Rabbi Luzzatto inspired many generations of Jews throughout Europe and the Near East. He especially believed that we must each structure our immediate social surroundings so as to maximize their salutatory effects upon us. Speaking from a perspective that aroused considerable excitement and innovative methods among *musar* leaders more than a century later, Rabbi Luzzatto recommended, "Each individual must guide and direct himself according to his calling and according to the particular activities in which he is engaged. In view of the fact that circumstances vary, it follows, of necessity, that the means by which they are to be directed towards the desired goal must vary in kind."

The intriguing notion that we must each develop specific strategies to ensure our inner growth has long been linked to traditional Jewish sentiment about the influence of habit on our personal makeup. For thousands of years, the sages have stressed that habit can lift us up to the loftiest realms of sainthood or pull us down to complete self-destruction. As we have noted earlier, the Talmud colorfully relates that the *yezer hara* begins as a fragile, lightly touching thread and ends as a strong wagon-rope that binds us. In a more optimistic expression of this same idea, the Talmud cogently comments that, "Learning becomes part of the very blood of him who learns in his youth."

Maimonides had much to say about the incalculable effects of habit upon the formation of adult personality. Many centuries before William James—the founder of American psychology—issued his famous pronouncement on habit as "the fly-wheel of society," Maimonides saw this force as inestimable in its importance for our own proper development. While he emphasized that we are born with the capacity for outstanding achievement in many realms, he regarded the role of habit—and the environment—as critical for self-realization:

Know that these moral virtues and vices are acquired and firmly established in the soul by frequently repeating the actions pertaining to a particular moral habit over a long period of time and by our becoming accustomed to them. If these actions are good, we shall acquire the virtue; if they are bad, we shall acquire the vice . . . . By nature, man . . . undoubtedly is habituated from childhood to actions in accordance with his family's way of life and that of the people in his town.

Maimonides also elaborated on how we can make specific use of habit to fortify our character. His ideas strikingly parallel the insights of modern behavioral psychology, for he recommended repetition as a key device. He also advised that individuals seek to attain the "harmonious mean" with respect to each of their inner qualities, such as diligence, self-discipline, or cheerfulness:

A man shall habituate himself in these character traits until they are firmly established in him. Time after time, he shall perform actions in accordance with the character traits that are in the man. He shall repeat them continually until performing them is easy ... . and firmly established in his soul.

In a consistent manner, Rabbi Luzzatto stressed that our higher capabilities—those of our *neshamah*—do not unfold automatically, as do our physical characteristics. In this respect, he would certainly disagree—as would Maimonides and his intellectual predecessors—with the more superficially optimistic psychological thinkers today who view self-improvement as a wholly spontaneous matter, like a flower budding in spring. Indeed, Rabbi Luzzatto affirmed earlier Jewish teachings that our impulses for growth are rather weak and require continual assistance for their triumph over our lower drives. He commented,

Sentiments of saintliness . . . are not so deeply rooted within a person so as to obviate the necessity of his employing certain devices in order to acquire them. In this respect, they differ from states such as sleep and wakefulness, hunger and satiety, and all other reactions which are stamped in one's nature, in that various methods and devices are perforce required for their acquisition.

In more recent times, both the Hasidic and *musar* founders accentuated this principle in their efforts to uplift others. For example, Rabbi Nachman of Bratslav contended again and again that we must rely upon special strategies to attain any real growth within. He argued that our ego cleverly thwarts most of our attempts at change and maturation—and that it is particularly skillful in neutralizing merely intellectual intentions. Thus he adopted music, storytelling, and other non-analytic methods to enable people to awaken spiritually. "As a general rule, to achieve anything holy, you must throw all your strength into it," Rabbi Nachman declared, "and use whatever ingenuity you can to succeed."

Several decades later, Rabbi Israel Salanter established the *musar* movement specifically to catalyze greater self-perfection among world Jewry. He shared the early Hasidic ideal of individual saint-hood, but vigorously opposed its zealous worship of a few particular leaders or *zaddikim*. In extolling the legendary exploits of the Baal Shem Tov and his original band of disciples, the Hasidim had lost sight of the necessity for improving their own, everyday conduct, he insisted. Indeed, Rabbi Salanter contended that Jews in the modern age needed to pay much closer attention to their day-to-day behavior in family life, business relations, and other pragmatic spheres. He felt that the rise of secularism and materialism in the West had done much to undermine traditional Jewish values; yet, he believed that some rapprochement with the scientific ethos was possible. In this regard, he viewed Maimonides an ideal for all.

Though Rabbi Salanter lived before the advent of scientific psychology, with its discovery of the unconscious, he evidenced an acute understanding of the problems inherent in any sustained effort at significant self-improvement. "It is more difficult to alter a single character trait than to cover the entire Talmud," he pointedly commented. Rabbi Salanter taught that our personal failures in life usually stem not from poor intentions, but from the inability to successfully implement our goals and aspirations. Few deliberately set out to underachieve, he observed, yet the vast majority of humanity realize only a fraction of their moral and intellectual potential. Consequently, the *musar* founder affirmed that specific strategies are absolutely essential to change this situation in the world.

### Aids to Self-Improvement

What concrete recommendations emerge from the lofty perspective of the Jewish sages? As we have already seen in passing, they have long emphasized that regular self-reflection is crucial for our inner well-being. The talmudic adage "He who ponders upon his conduct brings much good to himself" has been a foundation of Judaism. But the sages have been clear-eyed realists in observing that there is usually quite a gap between our best intentions and the reality of our daily behavior. We all know that New Year's resolutions seldom last beyond a day or two, though we are certainly sincere enough when we utter them. This phenomenon is scarcely new or a product of our hurried times, however; as far back as the third century C.E., *Pirkey Avoth* admonishes, "Do not say when I have leisure, I will study. Perhaps, you will have no leisure."

Even when we feel strongly committed to self-improvement, we are aware that something within us keeps postponing or delaying important matters we need to work on. An all-too-common tendency is to heed—gladly—the inner voice that says, "Wait until later in the day," or "Wait until later in the week," or "Wait until you have more time." Certainly this is one of the oldest means of procrastination. As Rabbi Luzzatto commented, "In reality, this is one of the clever devices of the evil inclination—to mount pressure unrelentingly against the hearts of men and to leave them no leisure to consider and observe the type of life they are leading." In our own fast-paced society, this comment seems especially germane.

Judaism has offered a practical solution to this dilemma: We must utilize habit as an aid rather than as a hindrance. That is, just as habit can pull us down into a day-to-day state resembling slumber, so can it elevate us to higher consciousness. Major Jewish thinkers have therefore advised that we make habit work for us, as one of the strategies necessary for effective self-advancement.

How is this to be accomplished? Rabbi Luzzatto stated the issue quite succinctly when he recommended, "Set aside a definite time for this weighing, so that it is not a fortuitous matter, but one which is conducted with the greatest regularity—for it yields rich concerns." In a like manner, the early Hasidic leaders stressed the usefulness of instituting inner stock-taking on a regularly scheduled basis. Rabbi Nachman, perhaps above all other Hasidic founders, emphasized that we cannot leave to casual circumstance the necessity for consistent self-examination. "You must therefore make sure—to set aside a specific time each day to calmly review your life," he advised. "Consider what you are doing and ponder whether it is worthy that you devote your life to it." There is no adequate alternative to this practice, he taught, for "One who does not meditate cannot have wisdom." Of course, a growing number of medical and therapeutic practioners today advocate precisely this point of view to ensure our mental and bodily well-being.

Historically, most Jewish sources prescribe such activity for the late evening hours. They have suggested that before we retire for the night, each of us mentally review all the day's events in a methodical way. Certainly, our sleep becomes less anxious and fitful as a result. The Kabbalists have practiced a somewhat more elaborate method—they sleep during the first hours of darkness and then awaken at midnight for meditation and sacred study. While there has been general agreement that nighttime is best suited for taking stock of ourselves, Jewish mystics have practiced more sustained efforts at enhancing their inward awareness. For instance, Rabbi Moses Cordovero, who lived in sixteenth-century Safed in Israel, instructed his disciples to reflect upon the day's events prior to eating each meal; such a procedure has obvious emotional and physical benefits. As Rabbi Luzzatto cogently remarked, "What emerges from all this is that a man must constantly—at all times, and particularly during a regularly appointed time of solitude— reflect upon the true path."

Jewish sages have further indicated that, in addition to scheduling a particular part of the day for elevating our state of mind, we can gain much from designing a particular room for this purpose. Once more, their underlying notion is that we must strive to use habit to our advantage as much as possible, for it can undermine even our finest intentions. If we become accustomed to personal stock-taking at a definite time and place every day, our progress will be greatly accelerated. Rabbi Nachman of Bratslav aptly observed, "It is very good to have a special room set aside for . . . [sacred] study and prayer [and] secluded meditation . . . . It is very good even to sit in such a special room. The atmosphere is beneficial, even if you just sit there and do nothing else." In our own era, the psychiatrist Carl Jung built a small stone cottage near his house for precisely such a "retreat." He would regularly cloister himself there for his far journeys into the inner world.

Another helpful aid to self-reflection, as major Jewish thinkers have advocated for centuries, is for individuals to keep a diary or journal to record their growth within. This practice seems to date far back to ancient times in Judaism. The Midrash relates that the biblical patriarch Jacob kept a log of the significant events in his life, including his son Joseph's provocative dreams. Another legend has it that a particular Recording Angel dwells in heaven. Sitting beneath the Tree of Life, he marks all that happens here on earth. In some Jewish tales, it is Elijah who took on this vital duty after his ascension to paradise; the Midrash also recounts that, "When a man is about to die, God appears to him and bids him to set down in writing all he has done during his life.'' Of course, a central theme of the Days of Awe is that each of us is annually judged as to our deeds, words, and thoughts—and the decision from above then inscribed in the Book of Life.

Over the centuries, many illustrious Jewish figures have recorded their dreams, as well as their waking thoughts, in personal journals. They have also typically copied inspiring quotations from Scripture, sacred commentaries, and even made note of chance remarks overheard in daily conversations with others. For example, Rabbi Joseph Karo—a legal genius and mystic in sixteenth-century Safed—kept for more than thirty years a diary of the ideas that came to him, reputedly from divine sources, when he entered trance-like mental states. Rabbi Chaim Vital, his contemporary, kept a detailed log of his dreams, as did Rabbi Nachman of Bratslav nearly three centuries later.

What should be the focus of our daily time for self-examination and our corresponding journal entries? Kabbalists have traditionally relied on rather abstruse visualization techniques to develop their powers of concentration and intentionality; they have also made use of dream interpretation and meditative exercises based on the letters of the Hebrew alphabet. However, as both Hasidic and *musar* leaders have insisted, we must devote adequate attention to our conduct each day—as a precursor to all more advanced inner work.

In this light, Rabbi Nachman of Bratslav advised a very interesting method for breaking unwanted habits. It involves visualization as a tool for self-transformation. With Rabbi Nachman's technique, we simply close our eyes and review each event of the day. When we come to an occurrence in which we feel that we acted foolishly, tensely, or improperly, we should then ''play back'' the situation— but this time, we visualize how we would like to have better handled that encounter. Eventually, Rabbi Nachman taught, we can develop powerful self-confidence and poise from this daily meditative technique. Later in this book we will explore a variety of exercises derived from Jewish tradition to aid in our inner development.

### Teachers and Friends

Historically, though, the sages have emphasized that a second set of guidelines is essential for effective self-growth; namely, those relating to our environment. In keeping with their longstanding belief that we are strongly influenced by our social surroundings, they have never advocated that we attempt to strengthen ourselves merely through solitary means. In fact, they have viewed such an outlook as misguided and even arrogant. ''A man sees no faults in himself'' has been the classic talmudic dictum on this issue.

As far back as *Pirkey Avoth*, Judaism is thus filled with references to the notion that only others can help us notice all of our own flaws; the task simply cannot be done alone. No matter how much *kavvanah*, or will, we bring to our soul-searching and meditating, we need assistance to examine our ''blind spots'' within. To enable us to accomplish this formidable task, the sages have stressed the importance of living in a supportive community, where higher values predominate. But they have also recognized that such communities are rare and can really exert only indirect effects. From their age-old perspective, then, the sages identify two essential requirements for a beneficial social environment: the active presence of a teacher or mentor, and the company of a trusted *haver*—a friend. We will look at each of these briefly in turn.

Throughout Jewish history, the role of the scholar or sage has been paramount. It is almost a truism to say that Judaism has revered the role of the teacher in our daily existence. Certainly, since the time of the destruction of the Second Temple in Jerusalem, the sages have occupied the most exalted status in Jewish regard. In talmudic days, they were not only venerated for their insights on leading a harmonious way of life, some were seen to possess divine powers. Legends in the *aggadah* and Midrash extol their ability to elicit rain from the skies, discern far-off events, or create living forms by uttering holy words. *Pirkey Avoth* declares repeatedly that each person needs to secure a personal teacher, as a fundamental principle of healthful living. ''Let your house be a meeting place for the wise,'' it advises, ''and sit amidst the dust of their feet and drink in their words with thirst.''

In the village world of Eastern Europe, the Hasidic founders placed tremendous emphasis on the value of finding the right teacher, or *rebbe*. They argued forcefully that achieving perfection of character is not possible wholly from books, even the sacred ones of Judaism. Much has to be learned from the heart, they insisted, and not just the intellect. With the suitable teacher, they taught, we can awaken our true, hidden potentials; we can fulfill our very purpose on earth. The Hasidim viewed the *zaddik*—the righteous "leader of the generation"—as an even loftier figure—one capable of influencing the very realms of heaven. As Rabbi Nachman of Bratslav therefore advised, "Draw close to the *Zaddikim* and walk in the paths they guide you along. Follow their teachings and then the truth will be inscribed within you . . . . This is how redemption will occur."

Many classic Hasidic tales celebrate the value of associating with such a mentor. Typically, these stories indicate that book knowledge is among the least important lessons to be gleaned from our real teachers in life. Thus one Hasid related that he sought out the Baal Shem Tov "to learn how he lights his pipe." Another Hasidic leader, who studied under the Maggid of Mezritch, recounted that he had come "to learn how he ties his shoelaces." Still another prominent Hasid related that, from his own master, he had above all "learned how to sleep properly."

Judaism however has never advocated the deification of even our most inspiring moral guides. Thus no religious festivals or holy days commemorate the births of the greatest Jewish leaders in history. Though we may venerate our personal teachers, the tradition admonishes us not to place them beyond the power of our own critical judgment. To do so has been seen to open the door to paganism, idolatory, and cultism. "Though all reverence and deference are due to one's teacher," the Talmud flatly states, "yet in the matter of censurable conduct, it becomes the pupil's duty to protest against it. Bad conduct is contaminating." The message is clear that, after all, the most lofty individual is still human.

Interestingly, the time-honored Jewish emphasis on having a personal mentor or role model is gaining strong validation in current psychology. Beginning in the early 1940s, Abraham Maslow devoted nearly thirty years to the study of people whom he termed "self-actualizing"—that is, men and women who truly seemed to make use of all their talents and abilities. Among Dr. Maslow's many significant findings was that the sheer company of such persons can be quite beneficial to others. He thus remarked during a lecture to those seeking greater fulfillment, "If you want to become self-actualizing, one of the best ways I know is to be around self-actualizing people. You can't help but be affected by them."

In the field of humanistic management, the importance of a

mentor for one's career development has likewise come to be recognized accurately. In the absence of an appealing role model to emulate, managerial studies suggest, many are likely to drift without a clear sense of inner goals. In fact, Dr. Maslow contended that an effective means to know someone's true personality is to ask who his or her exemplars or heroes are. To have none, he felt, is a sure sign of some disturbance in mental well-being.

As a second vital way to create a personally nuturing social environment, the sages have for centuries recommended that we find an appropriate friend with whom we can share the vicissitudes of life. While the major Jewish thinkers have certainly viewed the vertical relationship involving a mentor as highly desirable for self-improvement, they have also greatly valued this horizontal relationship between equals. For instance, *Pirkey Avoth* in the same sentence recommends both of these elements for building a harmonious existence for ourselves. "Procure yourself a teacher, acquire unto yourself an associate [*haver*], and judge all men in the scale of merit," it advises. In a similar manner, the Talmud suggests, "Get thee a companion, one to whom you can tell your secrets." More pointedly, the Talmud advises, "In choosing a friend, go up a step."

With their initially populist and anti-elitist orientation, the early Hasidic leaders regarded the assistance of a trusted confidant as an important asset in everyday living. In their many public discourses and writings, they stressed the unique benefits a person can reap from having an intimate acquaintance with whom to discuss moral and emotional concerns. "You should always talk to your friends about spiritual matters," Rabbi Nachman of Bratslav commented. Though an ardent mystic, he insisted that the seemingly mundane practice of sharing religious feelings or thoughts with another in a heartfelt way can be a very powerful means of self-transformation. Exotic forms of meditation are not always necessary, he taught; nor is it so important if our *haver* does not always see eye-to-eye with us:

Sometimes, when you speak to a friend about . . . [higher matters], your words are not accepted. Still, you can be motivated by your own words . . . . They may have had no effect if you had spoken them to yourself. But when you speak them to your friend . . . and he is not influenced, they are reflected back to you.

In their approach to counseling, the early *rebbes* relied extensively on this intriguing notion. They characteristically made sure that the Hasid's "spiritual confidant" was appraised of the specific guidance that had been given; thereupon, the *haver* was entrusted with the responsibility of serving as the *rebbe*'s surrogate, helping the individual to implement the advice on a day-to-day basis. Despite the *rebbe*'s awesome position in the Hasidic world, he knew that the Hasid's likelihood for real change within was far greater with a friend's active involvement.

In the nineteenth century, the *musar* movement elevated this concept to a central place in their approach to self-improvement. For example, some *yeshivot* incorporated an early version of dyad therapy—a modern, humanistic method embraced by Carl Rogers, Abraham Maslow, and other influential psychologists in our own time. In the *musar* technique, each *yeshiva* student was assigned a peer with whom to closely associate for the specific purpose of mutual help and support—both intellectually and emotionally. Sometimes, they would jointly seek methods of self-development. Strong, lifelong friendships often resulted from this arrangement; students learned to accept and even elicit helpful advice from others in this way.

Another provocative *musar* practice that antedates contemporary group therapy or encounter groups also bears mention. Small numbers of students would regularly meet for informal but earnest discussion; in a group atmosphere of friendship and equality, they would examine one another's conduct over recent days and offer constructive criticism and suggestions for improvement. The group was run democratically, with an older student serving as chairperson.

In another innovative *musar* method, each *yeshiva* student was instructed to meditate at least once per week on the biblical commandment, "Love your neighbor as yourself." But the goal was not simply to help the individual focus certain thoughts more clearly; concrete deeds were expected too. Thus the student was encouraged each week to carry out the mitzvah of loving-kindness or altruism (*gemiluth hesed*) by performing some selfless act of service for a fellow student or member of the community.

It is important to realize that the psychological model that underlies such strategies for self-improvement is one that extols our innate capacities for growth and change. Indeed, Rabbi Salanter and his disciples argued vigorously that any person can alter any character trait at any time—provided he or she genuinely seeks the desired goal. In contrast to the dominant, twentieth-century perspective that has focused almost exclusively on the flaws and disturbances of human personality, the *musar* founders and their precursors in Judaism have always emphasized our highest possibilities for growth and achievement. In this sense, their outlook seems especially relevant today, with the rising interest in our creative potentials and loftier motivations in life.

Throughout the millennia, Jewish sages have contended that much effort is necessary for personal development. To awaken greater creative and intuitive strength will not happen overnight, they have taught; ultimately, we are each held responsible for fulfilling our inner capacities. Thus Maimonides plainly stated, "Therefore, it is obligatory . . . that [one] be avid and work hard for his own sake, to acquire the virtues, since there is no one outside of himself moving him toward them." Alluding to Hillel's classic precept, Maimonides thereupon commented, "This is what they say in the moral teachings . . . 'If I am not for myself, who will be?'" In a consistent manner, Rabbi Luzzatto rhetorically asked his readers, "How will our thoughts be purified, if we do not rescue them from [their] imperfections?"

Nevertheless, Jewish thought affirms that we must climb the celestial ladder carefully and methodically. As Rabbi Nachman of Bratslav poetically explained, we can become quite misled if we are overhasty. "When a building burns down, people often rescue the most worthless items. Do not do the same in your confusion," he aptly advised.

In short, each rung on the ladder that Jacob beheld exists for a purpose; no real shortcuts are possible. When we are guided by this awareness, our ascent to the divine will be surrounded in true splendor.

3

# Spiritual Exercises

# 5

# TAKING STOCK

In the bustle of modern society, nearly all of us occasionally feel beset and beleaguered by external pressures. Even when we possess a strong sense of purpose, the clamor of our era can sometimes seem deafening and overwhelming. When that event occurs, we find it hard to hear the ''still small voice'' within—the Source of all our strength. For some people, the surrounding din has become so pervasive and habitual that there appears no respite. In either situation, it is vital for us to pause and look at ourselves closely: our values, our relationships, and our inner direction.

Such a prescription for wholeness, of course, is not a new invention; Judaism has always recognized the importance of periodic soul-searching—so much so, in fact, that the Jewish calendar specifies a special time for it during the year. Historically, the month of Ellul—that is, the twenty-eight days prior to the onset of Rosh Hashanah—and the ten days between Rosh Hashanah and Yom Kippur—have been specifically allocated to deep self-scrutiny or *heshbon nefesh*. In this way, the Days of Awe become each year an opportunity for drawing closer to the divine; the spiritual power they possess can then be felt in full splendor.

The sages have also designated the weekly Sabbath as a special day for personal awakening, not just a day to refrain from material concerns. For example, they have characteristically offered on Sabbath afternoons their most provocative discourses concerning our hidden potential and the nature of the universe. In short, the tradition of regular stock-taking within is a time-honored one in Judaism.

This process, though, has always been seen as manifesting on many levels simultaneously. The Kabbalah teaches that our psyche is vast and complex, containing worlds upon worlds. In fact, the human mind is said to mirror the awesome structure of the entire cosmos. By venturing inward, you may therefore come to understand not only your own makeup, but the mysteries of the universe as well. As the thirteenth-century *Zohar* concisely observes, "Man is fashioned as a microcosm of the world."

Consequently, the spiritual exercises in this chapter have two key purposes. The first is to help you map your present existence within the sacred coordinates of space, time, and experience. You will be encouraged to explore the parameters of your strengths and talents, flaws, and inner heights. And you will be asked to take a reckoning as to the major influences upon you. For—paradoxical as it seems— according to the Jewish tradition, you can find your true Self only by identifying the location of others in your life—as teachers, guides, *zaddikim*, and hidden saints. Having carried out these steps, you will then be in an optimal position to envision and fulfill your personal goals, thereby creating your own "paradise on earth."

I recommend that you devote adequate time to each specific exercise. As mentioned earlier in this book, major Jewish thinkers have typically kept a journal to record their spiritual growth. I therefore strongly advise that you begin one of your own; as you carry out these exercises, make careful note of your answers. The sequence of the exercises should also be observed, as it follows the states of *heshbon nefesh* outlined by Hillel the Elder close to two thousand years ago.

Ideally, you might spend perhaps a Sabbath afternoon in quiet self-reflection upon a single exercise. Or, you may find that you prefer to begin one but complete it over a period of several days, as new thoughts come to you. The effects of each exercise are subtle yet powerful; consequently, you may wish to space them at least a few days or two weeks apart.

In accordance with the various changes in your life, you will probably discover that your answers to the questions posed will likewise shift into new patterns of meaning. However, quite important feelings or insights may quickly arise out of this activity; such responses should also be incorporated into your journal.

While these exercises are mainly intended for individual involvement, they may be useful too in group settings, such as spiritual retreats and *havurah* encounters. In these instances, it would be helpful to have a leader familiar with group dynamics and processes. You may also find it rewarding to share these exercises jointly with someone you love.

### Exercise 1. If I Am Not for Myself, Who Will Be?

We often go through life as our own worst enemies, berating ourselves for matters we would easily forgive in others. Or, we dwell solely on our inner flaws and seeming failures, rarely taking credit for our genuine triumphs and achievements. This pattern of thought can be quite self-defeating. As the Hasidic founders repeatedly stressed, we must always recall that each of us is ultimately connected to the highest reaches of the divine.

For instance, the Baal Shem Tov declared, "Forgetfulness is exile. Remembrance is redemption." His great-grandson, Rabbi Nachman of Bratslav, similarly remarked, "Man includes all the worlds. There is nothing beyond his ability." Rabbi Nachman used to advise that when we want to help another person change for the better, we should focus on his strengths and talents—and use these as building blocks for new traits. He pointedly observed that our greatest barrier to true self-development lies in our tendency to belittle ourselves. Rabbi Israel Salanter, originator of the *musar* movement, espoused this same outlook. Both figures, therefore, advocated that any effort at self-improvement must begin with an encouraging look at our "best" personality features.

In this exercise, first list as many of your positive character traits as possible. Be objective; look at yourself as if you were an outsider. Avoid false modesty here; you are entitled to feel good and happy about your admirable qualities—especially as such an awareness can help spur you forward to further inner attainment.

Second, beside each trait you list, describe an actual event in your life that shows the characteristic in action. For example, if you have listed honesty as a trait, indicate in a few sentences an episode that clearly demonstrated this quality.

Third, list the five most important accomplishments of your life—not necessarily by anyone else's standards, but by your own. If you wish, you may rank these items from the first most significant achievement—in your eyes—to the fifth.

Finally, identify the various activities in your day-to-day existence that give you the strongest sense of personal well-being, happiness, and fulfillment. Be as specific as possible; try to list at least five. These should all be involvements that you engage in fairly frequently throughout the year, rather than rare or exotic occurrences. The next section will focus on these latter experiences.

As the Hasidic master Rabbi Ber of Lublin reminds us, "Each one must see to which way he is attracted, and in this way, he is to serve with all his strength."

### Exercise 2. *Above the Maze*

At certain moments in our lives, something happens and we suddenly feel exalted beyond our ordinary frame of mind. The catalyzing event may be outwardly quite mundane, even trivial; or it may mark an exciting, rare occasion—such as the birth of a child. But what seems to matter most is that we thereby gain a powerful perspective on who we are and what our purpose is on earth. From this inward state, we become far more able to form and institute far-reaching changes around us. We look at things from our *neshamah*, our Higher Self, and not from our lower impulses.

In the early eighteenth century, the young Italian mystic Rabbi Moses Chaim Luzzatto poetically described these occurrences and their importance. In his book *Mesillat Yesharim* (*The Path of the Just*), an ethical guide beloved to succeeding generations of Jews, he observed:

Daily life [is like] . . . a garden maze . . . [with] many conflicting and interlacing paths, all similar to one another, the purpose of the whole being to challenge one to reach a portico in the midst . . . . The walker between the paths has no way of seeing or knowing whether he is on the true or the false path; for they are all similar . . . . He who occupies a commanding position in the portico, however, sees all of the paths before him and can discriminate between the true and the false one.

Yet, as Rabbi Luzzatto and many other brilliant thinkers have noted, it is unfortunately quite common for such wondrous moments to fade from conscious memory and even lose their impact altogether. The view from the portico is indeed striking, but most of the time we can catch it only in glimpses. On this intriguing subject, Rabbi Nachman of Bratslav remarked—perhaps somewhat poignantly—"You may have a vision, but even with yourself you cannot share it. Today, you may be inspired and see a new light. But tomorrow, you will no longer be able to communicate it, even to yourself."

For this reason, it is vital for us to recall and identify those episodes in which we gain an unusual sense of clarity and purpose about our lives. That way, we can once again attain a crucial vantage point from which to see what really endows our existence with personal meaning.

In this exercise, describe as many of these specific occurrences as possible from within your past experience. Looking back over the years, can you recall when you have felt closest to God or the *Ein Sof*, the Infinite? In what experience have you tasted true awe? Ecstasy? A sense of something truly miraculous or holy? Specify the circumstances surrounding the event, particularly what seemed to have catapulted you "above the maze" of everyday life, into new heights of consciousness.

Next, answer these questions: How did your world appear to you during each happening? How did you feel inside? And, if any feelings or thoughts came to you concerning your "mission" in life, what were these?

### *Exercise 3 Wealth*

Ours has often been called the Age of Anxiety. Despite a material affluence that would have seemed dazzling and incredible to our ancestors just a few generations ago, many people find that chronic tension is an inescapable feature of their daily lives. As evidenced by the millions of people who each night require a chemical sedative in order to fall asleep, we do not easily let go of our insecurities.

Yet, this phenomenon is not simply an outgrowth of modern, technological conditions. Nearly two thousand years ago, at the time of the Second Temple of Jerusalem, Ben Zoma declared, "Who is wealthy? He who rejoices in his lot. Who is honored? He who honors his fellow man." Nearer to our own day, in the *shtetls* of Eastern Europe, a popular folk saying observed, "While pursuing happiness, we flee from contentment."

Throughout the centuries, Jewish tales and legends have highlighted the impermanence and instability of the material sphere. Rabbi Nachman of Bratslav used to compare the world to a spinning Hannukah *dreidl*, with all revolving from high to low. On one level, he intended his richly symbolic stories to dramatize the foolishness of attaching too much importance to superficial trappings around us.

According to the Midrash, even the great King Solomon of the Bible was cast down from his exalted position and forced to wander for several years as a tattered beggar. By taking his blessings for granted, he became arrogant and was then judged from on high as deserving of this sobering experience. Solomon was obliged to trudge across the boundaries of kingdoms and wearily ponder his previous thoughtlessness until his penitence was complete.

In the Hasidic era, the *rebbes* used to tell a variety of stories on the nature of riches. In an anonymous legend about the Baal Shem Tov, a wealthy man boasts of his ample possessions and asks the Hasidic founder for a similar status in the World to Come. The Besht imparts some specific business advice, which the man eagerly seeks to carry out. In doing so, he quickly experiences a sequence of devastating events that reduce him to utter ruin. Humbled and penniless, he returns amidst a group of supplicants visiting the Baal Shem Tov. Thereupon the sage restores the man's affluence, which he now sees in its proper perspective.

In our own time, many of Isaac Bashevis Singer's alluring stories underscore this same theme: True wealth lies within—the rest may be quite transitory. In one characteristic tale, a renowned but complacent author is en route to an international speaking engagement. Through a disastrous series of accidents—encompassing the terrible vagaries of the weather to poor communications among people— the famous author suddenly finds himself dependent for sheer physical survival on a simple stranger's kindness.

In this exercise, identify and describe all the key "blessings" over the course of your life to date. List at least ten, if possible. Begin with your childhood and origins; continue your list up through the present. Then answer these questions: Which of these aspects of good fortune have been transient for you? Which have been permanent? What have been your greatest inner possessions? What has your "wealth" consisted of at various times in your life—and what does it consist of now? Be as specific as possible in all your responses.

*Exercise 4. Descent into Egypt*

According to Jewish tradition, there are four distinct ways to understand the narratives of the Bible. The letters of the Hebrew word *Pardes* (often translated as "Paradise"), we are told, contain the clue to the secret contained therein: P represents *Peshat*, the simple, exterior meaning of the passage; R stands for *Remez*, the homiletical meaning; D is *Drush*, the allegorical meaning; and S is *Sod*, its most hidden, recondite meaning.

Alluding to this intriguing concept, the *Zohar* plainly warns us, "Woe unto those who see in the Law nothing but simple accounts and ordinary words! . . . Every word of the Law contains an elevated sense and a sublime mystery."

Historically, therefore, the sages have explained the story of Abraham's "descent into Egypt" as signifying on one level a journey into the depths of his own "Egypt" within. His mission? To elevate his lower impulses, thereby transforming these into instruments of divine power. In this light, the opening words of that biblical section, *"Lech Lekha"* ("Go Out"), have traditionally been interpreted to mean, "Go out—to yourself"—the heavenly command to Abraham.

Closer to our own era, many Hasidic parables poetically illustrate the important psychological principle that even our worst flaws can be raised upward and directed to beneficial purposes in daily life. For example, the Hasidic leader Rabbi Wolf of Zabaraz was once told that some Jews in his town had spent the whole night at the gambling table. He thereupon remarked, "Perhaps, it is their intention to accustom themselves to the habit of remaining awake all night. After they acquire this habit, they may learn to devote the whole night to holy study and divine service."

In a like manner, Rabbi Israel Salanter often spoke of the need to "transmute" our more primitive desires—originating in the *yezer hara*—into productive and useful forces. He recommended that we each allocate a definite time each day to this vital aspect of self-development.

In this exercise, like Abraham, you must therefore initiate a journey into the far regions of your own "Egypt." That is, what sorts of negative attitudes, beliefs, and behavioral patterns currently exist there? List the personality traits that you recognize as least appealing in your present internal makeup. Be as honest and objective as possible, once more looking at yourself as might an outsider.

Beside each trait that you identify—, for example, being quick-tempered or too judgmental of others—describe in a few sentences a recent event that revealed the presence of that flaw within you. Explore the terrain of your inner "Egypt" as fully as possible.

Finally, indicate with each example how you might have acted instead, so that your higher capabilities—those of your *neshamah* might have been strengthened. Be specific. You may find it helpful to practice here Rabbi Nachman of Bratslav's powerful technique. That is, visualize yourself in the exact same situation you have just pictured, but now picture yourself behaving in a more praiseworthy manner. If you practice this method, its results may pleasantly surprise you.

### *Exercise 5. Teachers of the Way*

Judaism has always stressed that we need other people to guide us properly through the straits of life. No one is expected to develop personal strengths in isolation from family, friends, and community. Without the crucial benefit of living teachers and role models, we would find it nearly impossible to gain the knowledge necessary for making successful decisions.

For instance, *Pirkey Avoth*, which dates back nearly eighteen hundred years, repeatedly extols the advantages we acquire in having superb teachers. Over and over this key text emphasizes that we should do all we can to find a true teacher for ourselves. Thus *Pirkey Avoth* indicates that Rabbi Joshua ben Parachia advised, "Get yourself a teacher and acquire unto yourself an associate, and judge all men in the scale of merit." His near contemporary, Rabbi Joseph ben Joezer, similarly recommended, "Let your house be a meeting place for the wise . . . and drink in their words with thirst."

Many centuries later, the Hasidic founders placed great insistence on this important notion. They considered the term *moreh derekh* (teacher of the Way) to be one of the highest epithets a person could use in referring to his or her *rebbe*. Indeed, many Hasidic tales celebrate how Hasidim developed key inner qualities by observing their *rebbes* perform such apparently trivial acts as lighting a pipe, getting dressed, or even sleeping.

In this exercise, review your own life to date. Who have been your most important teachers in the broadest sense of the term? Perhaps at the time you did not recognize them as such, but you are now observing from this moment's special vantage point. Who has helped awaken your higher sensitivities, interests, talents, and potentials? List as many of these teachers of the Way as you can—five at the very least—going back to your childhood up through the present. They may certainly have been family members and friends, as well as those involved in a more formal relationship with you. And they may literally have been teachers of some field of knowledge or creative activity.

After each individual's name you record, describe what he or she taught you—that is, what particular lessons, insights, or skills you learned from the person, or what you are learning at present.

Having completed this exercise, you may wish to contact each person, if still alive, and express your gratitude. However, if this act is not possible, then an inward expression of gratitude might be appropriate.

### Exercise 6.   From All Things

The sages of the Jewish people have long advised us to benefit not only from those who lead obviously exemplary lives. We are in fact urged to gain knowledge from everyone—even from those who outwardly would seem to have little to offer us.

In *Pirkey Avoth*, we are therefore reminded, "Ben Zoma said, 'Who is wise? He that learns from all men.' . . . Ben Azzai said, 'Despise not any man and discard not anything, for there is not a man who has not his hour and there exists not a thing which has not its place.' "

The talmudic sages strongly elevated this notion in their teachings. Extolling the daily world as a place filled with opportunities for self-development, they explicitly commented that we can even learn important lessons in life from observing the animals in their natural ways—such as industriousness from the ant and modesty from the cat.

The early Hasidic leaders emphasized this outlook through their many parables and stories. Based on the central message of the Baal Shem Tov that divine sparks are lodged in all things—yearning to be uplifted back to their Source—the *rebbes* advised their followers to recognize the hidden worth of all that occurs to them.

"The wise man learns from every phrase he hears, from every event he observes, and from every experience he shares," declared the Kobriner *Rebbe*. In a similar manner, Rabbi Nachman of Bratslav recommended that we seek the positive side to all situations. In this manner, he contended, "You will be able to use every experience as a means of drawing closer to God."

Consistent with this provocative idea, his colleagues presented aphorisms on what the attentive can learn from children and chess players, gamblers and musicians, acrobats and soldiers, and many other colorful characters encountered in the everyday world. The Maggid of Mezritch—chief disciple of the Besht—once even expounded on the seven higher lessons that a thief can teach us.

In this exercise, think back over the course of your life to those who have been your teachers through negative example. These may be individuals whom you very much disliked at the time, or who even repelled you by their attitude and conduct. Perhaps you still harbor feelings of anger or resentment toward them. Or, they may rather be people who entangled you in circumstances that you found quite unpleasant or disturbing. But with the loftier realization that each has in some way been a guide, list at least five such figures in your life, from childhood onward.

Beside each name, indicate what particular lesson you have learned as a result of your seemingly negative involvement with this person. Be as specific as possible. Finally, identify how you might have gained the same knowledge or insight through some other experience.

*Exercise 7. The Lamed-Vovniks* (Thirty-Six Hidden Saints)

One of the oldest and most profound Jewish legends is that of the thirty-six hidden just men, known in Yiddish as the *Lamed-vovniks* (*lamed-vov* means "thirty-six" in Hebrew). Tradition has taught that in every generation, the world itself is sustained by these secret saints. As the Talmud records the evocative words of the fourth-century Babylonian Jew, Abaye, these exalted personages "daily receive the Divine Countenance."

In some intriguing tales that have come down through the centuries, it is told that each one of these holy figures knows the identity of all the others. In this way, they form a hidden network—a cabal—that spans the continents. In other stories, it is said that no member is even aware of his own supernal role, let alone that of his peers. But common to all variants of the legend is the notion that these mighty saints are outwardly quite ordinary, engaged in the most mundane occupations—a cobbler, a water-carrier, a teacher of small children. Yet, the simplest act of the *Lamed-vovnik* is seen to exert incalculable effects on others.

For instance, it is said that a certain village tanner in the early Hasidic era was a *Lamed-vovnik*; after his death, this apparently ignorant fellow was discovered to have composed secret and sophisticated kabbalistic treatises. Two seemingly uneducated ritual slaughterers in another tiny Eastern European *shtetl* were likewise found after their deaths to have written—unbeknownst to their neighbors—erudite metaphysical texts that only the most learned could comprehend. Released from the conceit that accompanies fame, such exalted persons are in this manner able to carry out most effectively their sacred mission.

Perhaps, you have already encountered some or even all of these thirty-six "hidden just men." Possibly, you have even suspected that an individual whom you met was far more than he—or she— appeared to be at the time.

In this exercise, think back over the course of your life and identify those people who, through the kindness, simplicity, and quiet serenity displayed to you—and others—may have been secret *Lamed-vovniks*. Focus on your present circumstances and look for possibilities. Remember that flamboyance has never been their style; you may therefore have to stimulate your memory and awareness a bit. You may not be able to list all thirty-six—yet—but name as many as you can.

You may also wish to assume that, at all times, there is at least one *Lamed-vovnik* secretly operating in your life. If so, who is he or she right now?

### Exercise 8. *Zaddikim* and Heroes

In recent years, a growing number of social observers have commented on the disappearance of genuine heroes in the outlook of modern-day Western culture. That is, while heroic men and women certainly exist today, the very concept of personal heroism or greatness has somehow become suspect, or old-fashioned, and seemingly even obsolete. Undoubtedly, we live in a time of almost unprecedented cynicism.

Indeed, the last few decades have witnessed the emergence of a new social phenomenon—the ''anti-hero''—typically, an isolated man on the run, estranged from family, friends, community, himself, and the divine. With such models constantly thrust before the public eye, it is hardly surprising that we begin to doubt even the possible existence of *zaddikim*, the truly righteous.

Judaism, of course, has always insisted that our inner development vitally depends on our recognizing and learning from the spiritual giants who walk the earth. Even on their simplest level, the stories of the Bible are designed to offer us relevant exemplars in the form of Abraham and Sarah, Moses and Aaron, the Judges and Prophets, the Kings and other holy figures. The Talmud and Midrash are likewise filled with narratives that celebrate the deeds of exalted sages, as well as those of biblical personages. ''The world says that you should not seek greatness,'' declared the Hasidic leader Rabbi Nachman of Bratslav. ''But I say that you should seek only greatness—the greatest possible *Zaddik*.''

The major Jewish thinkers have contended that we can benefit immensely from simply learning abut heroic men and women of bygone days. Their influence is not seen to dim with the mere passage of the years. For example, the Talmud is written in the present tense as it cites the opinions or ''discussions'' of various scholars—often separated by entire continents and centuries. One Talmudic sage may raise an issue, and it will be answered by one who lived many years before. Thus, consistent with time-honored Jewish sentiment, Rabbi Nachman of Bratslav remarked that, ''Two men who live in different places, or even in different generations, may still converse.''

Indeed, few of us have not had the experience of feeling that some book written long ago speaks exactly to our innermost thoughts—or that a historically famous man or woman of the past expressed convictions that very much inspire us today.

In this exercise, give thought as to which people in the world—those either alive today or in the past, recent or otherwise—you most admire for their greatness. List all those whom you have aspired to be like in some way, or have sought to emulate in your own sphere of activity. These personal *zaddikim* can be world-renowned, or they may be unknown except to you and a handful of others with specific interests. But each figure must in your estimation embody some truly outstanding quality. Name as many people as you can and indicate in a sentence or two what you venerate most about each one.

### Exercise 9. *Tikkun* (Rectification)

Jewish mystics have long taught that holy sparks of Light are lodged in all things. In order for the act of Creation to occur, shards of the divine fell into the world of matter. Thus, as Rabbi Isaac Luria described this cosmic situation, it is the task of each person to redeem and liberate the sacred that lies within every material form, animate and inanimate. From stones and plants to animals, ourselves, and one another—a heavenly Exile exists until the Light returns unbroken to its Source.

For this reason, the kabbalists tell us, we are presented daily with innumerable opportunities for *tikkun*, or universal rectification. Through our *kavvanah* (intentionally) and *devekuth* (devotion), we literally help restore the supreme harmony. "The world is rectified only by man," insisted Rabbi Moses Chaim Luzzatto. "Man was given the task of rectifying all of Creation." On this same provocative subject, the Hasidic founder Rabbi Levi Yitzchok remarked, "Man must therefore raise up these sparks, elevating them higher and higher."

Yet, this process of divine rectification is not always visible to us on the obvious level. In fact, the Jewish mystical tradition emphasizes that we can never know the ultimate consequences of our deeds, words, or even thoughts; every aspect of the cosmos is considered to be inextricably connected to all others, and the effects of a single gesture or remark may be incalculable. The *Zohar* clearly informs us that, "The world at large consists of a hierarchy of created things . . . which literally form one organic body."

Many compelling Hasidic tales speak precisely to this point. In such stories, a man or woman may not only have to undergo various hardships, but also several lifetimes on earth, in order to carry out the proper *tikkun* for a thoughtless word, an unkind action, or an unexpressed emotion. Legend has it that the Baal Shem Tov would sometimes send a penitent Hasid into temporary exile, to enable him to redress successfully some fallen aspect of his life.

In this exercise, give thought to and identify what you need to rectify within your present sphere of activity. These may be subtle disharmonies to which you have contributed, or which you are simply aware of in others around you. Or, they might involve more serious imbalances that have continued for quite some time.

Specifically, then, what are the fallen sparks of Light in your social world that you are capable of redeeming? Have any relationships been left dangling due to a matter not fully discussed or glossed over? Do any actual misunderstandings need to be resolved? These may encompass the domain of family and friends, neighbors, people you work with, and others.

Next, as you look over the course of your entire life today, what "unfinished business" has yet to be completed? Perhaps a friendship was suddenly severed, or an interest abruptly dropped. Be as specific as possible in your answers. Remember, until such matters are rectified, you will be unable to truly embark on new opportunities and challenges.

### Exercise 10. Divine Providence

How can we know when we are truly following our path in life? It is certainly not always easy to foretell the outcome of a major decision we make; the essence of life seems indeed to be choice, yet sometimes we feel badly in need of a higher wisdom to guide us.

For many centuries, Jewish mystics have emphasized that one key source is always available to us. Known as Divine Providence, it is visible through the workings of meaningful coincidences in our everyday existence. For in the kabbalistic perspective, nothing that ever happens is really random or without purpose. Adepts have therefore long recommended that we seek the meaning behind apparently accidental events as a message communicated to us from beyond the mundane world.

For example, Rabbi Moses Chaim Luzzatto commented in *The Way of God*, "Things can happen to an individual both as an end in themselves and as a means toward something else . . . . Everything is ultimately decreed with the utmost precision, according to what is truly best." Several decades later, Rabbi Zussya, the Hasidic leader, put the matter quite poetically. "While the strands of cause and effect are being unraveled," he observed, "we grope about, calling things good and evil. What first appears as evil fortune, may discover itself, years later, as the best of events and a cause for rejoicing."

Many Hasidic tales are designed to impart this intriguing notion. In a representative story, the Baal Shem Tov is one day walking between two adjoining houses in the town of Nemerov. He suddenly finds that he has strayed into a cellar.

"Examine the *mezzuzos* of this cellar!" he commands. "The owner may be in terrible danger unless they are corrected!"

"If you lose your way and find yourself in a strange cellar, must you blame it on a particular cause? Can't it be attributed to mere coincidence?" his companion asks bewilderedly. The owner of the house inspects the *mezzuzos* and discovers that they have indeed become unfit.

"You see," comments the Besht, "there are no coincidences upon this earth."

In our own era, the Swiss psychiatrist Carl Jung articulated in detail the nature of this uncanny phenomenon, which he related to the principle of synchronicity. In such occurrences, he suggested, the very forces of space and time lose their boundaries or become relativistic. "Synchronicity takes the coincidence of events in space and time as meaning something more than mere chance," he declared. In his later years, Jung argued that the better able we are to discern and respond to startling coincidences, the more successful our judgments and choices. He also pointed out—similarly to Jewish mystics—that the greater our openness to encountering coincidences, the more frequently we appear to experience them.

In this exercise, describe those occurrences over the course of your life in which Divine Providence seemed to have been operative. List as many of these intriguing events as you can, when you happened to be "in the right place at the right time."

To what extent did each of these happenings change or influence your inner direction? Be as specific as possible. After describing each key "coincidence," try to recall and note your frame of mind before the event occurred.

### Exercise 11    Paradise

The Jewish mystical tradition teaches that much of what we experience in daily existence stems from our own attitudes and desires. We are advised that, in countless ways, both discernible and hidden, each of our acts, words, and even thoughts leaves its indelible imprint on the universe. "Everything is dependent on man's free will," the *Zohar* cogently explains "In truth, a man by his actions is always drawing to himself . . . good or evil, according to the path which he treads."

This central kabbalistic notion—that we actually fashion our own reality around us—became a key notion among the early Hasidim. The Hasidic founders often expounded through colorful folktales and parables upon this important concept. To the dissatisfied who yearned for external salvation in the World to Come, or for an earthly miracle to change their situation, such thinkers preached the esoteric doctrine that there is an unbroken continuity between this world and the next. Our innermost outlook ultimately forms the events that we physically experience, they taught.

In a beautiful Hasidic story that emphasizes this point, a man dreams that he has died and gone to heaven. He is judged as to the quality of his earthly life and is at last permitted to enter the celestial gates. Much to his surprise, he finds a familiarly simple, *shtetl*-like house of study, where he sees the greatest sages of Jewish history deeply absorbed in sacred study.

"Is this all there is?" the man exclaims. "I thought this was Paradise!"

Thereupon, a heavenly voice gently informs him, "Foolish one, the sages are not in Paradise. Paradise is in the sages."

More tersely, the Maggid of Mezritch—chief disciple of the Baal Shem Tov—once declared, "Each person creates his own Paradise. The reverse is [also] true."

In this exercise, use your imagination to the fullest. In as much space as you need, describe your own vision of Paradise on earth. What would it be like for you—and, perhaps, for others? Who would be there? How would it differ, if at all, from what you experience now in life? Make this account as personal as possible.

*Exercise 12. If Not Now, When?*

Once we have gained a clear sense of personal direction and purpose in life, our goals become far easier to attain. Not only may we move through our days more efficiently, but we find ourselves experiencing fortuitous "coincidences"—the workings of Divine Providence—more frequently. Nevertheless, it is not enough merely to think about the changes we wish to see; they must be actualized through concrete acts.

Judaism has always highlighted the importance of everyday activity as the means to inner advancement. Even its mystical side has contained this principle; the kabbalists teach us that of the four universes which exist, ours is the realm of *Assiyah*, or Action, where actual deeds are paramount. For this reason, the *Zohar*, the bible of Jewish mysticism, contends that, "In all things, some action is required to arouse the activity above."

Of course, we know that even with the most sincere intentions to act, we often procrastinate for long periods of time. Despite our well-formulated plans, we sometimes convince ourselves to wait a day or two, and another day or two, and so on until we lose all our momentum and inner resolve. This psychological problem, however, is hardly a product of modern times. Nearly two thousand years ago, Hillel the Elder astutely declared, "Do not say, 'When I have leisure, I will study.' Perhaps, you will have no leisure."

With acute recognition of this human tendency, the early Hasidic leaders offered much practical guidance on how to overcome inertia within. "Man's world consists of nothing except the day and hour he stands in now," Rabbi Nachman of Bratslav advised his followers. "Tomorrow is a completely different world." On another occasion, he declared on this same issue, "Yesterday and tomorrow do not exist."

The intent of this exercise, therefore is not to conjure up idle daydreams, but to help you focus—now—on what you need to fulfill your divine purpose. First, look inward and identify as precisely as possible what you would like to be doing with your life a decade from now. Describe your ideal situation, however optimistic or remote it may seem at present. Be as specific as you can.

Next, describe what you would like your situation to be five years from today, two years from today, and a year from now. Within the realistic constraints of each time period, imagine the most perfect sphere of activity for yourself. That is, if all were to go flawlessly for you, what would your life be like at each juncture of time?

Finally, what prevents you—right now—from realizing each of the four scenarios you have described? After each description, specify exactly what you need to do to begin the actualization of your dreams. What actions must you undertake? What steps do you need to carry out? What other events must happen? In meditating upon your course of action, bear in mind Rabbi Nachman's words: "The key to everything is the way you start."

Or, as the Hasidic leader Rabbi Yerachmiel recommended, "Start in a modest way, maintain an earnest effort to aspire higher and higher realms, and [eventually] . . . you shall have attained undreamed-of heights."

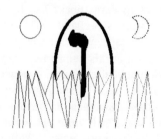

# 6

# OPENING THE GATES

We live in an age in which our inner world has often been demeaned and denigrated. The dominant scientific models of the human mind portray us as little better than the most savage of beasts, or as ultimately nothing more than complicated DNA-based machines. It is no wonder that many people today feel powerless and unable to effect real changes in their lives; they have been sold a false bill of goods, convincing them that the human individual is a passive, helpless creature, buffeted by social forces.

Such a picture, of course, leads to a destructive, self-fulfilling prophecy: If you genuinely believe that you can exert only meager influence on the course of your life, events will indeed seem random and chaotic. If you feel that your present situation, however unsatisfying, was long ago determined by circumstances beyond your control, you will certainly find innumerable obstacles standing in the way of your dreams. In short, as Rabbi Nachman of Bratslav observed, "A person's entire destiny—for good or ill—depends on the thoughts in his heart."

It is clear that the Jewish visionary tradition has long offered a vista of the human psyche far broader than that glimpsed through laboratory windows. For many centuries, its sages have taught that our powers within are virtually limitless—and that our own mental "slumber" prevents us from utilizing more of our vast, inborn potentials.

These provocative thinkers have repeatedly emphasized that our deepest, core impulses lead us to what we experience in daily existence. As we have seen, they have particularly stressed that imagination and intentionality are two key tools by which we can literally fashion our higher aspirations into the fabric of physical reality.

To do so necessitates definite, systematic practice. Like our other lofty traits, these must be recognized and then fortified through conscious effort. Otherwise, such crucial qualities for our well-being may remain weak and almost inert for many years. Thus Rabbi Nachman of Bratslav used to preach that people can go through an entire lifetime in a state of inner sleep or "constricted consciousness." In our own day, the present Lubavitcher *rebbe*, Rabbi Menachem M. Schneersohn, has commented that, "depending on how much the imaginative faculty is properly developed . . . [our success in life is partly based]. Likewise, without sufficient *kavvanah* or willpower to concentrate on our goals, we become easily impeded by the countless distractions that surround us every day.

The meditative exercises in this chapter are all intended to give you new vitality and creativity in mastering the challenges of your everyday life. Specifically, they are designed to help strengthen your faculties of imagination and *kavvanah* . . . the latter encompassing both concentration and intentionality. The images and themes are drawn from many time-honored sources within Judaism, including the Talmud, Midrash, and key kabbalistic works such as the *Zohar*. For many centuries, these motifs have served to nourish and elevate the Jewish spirit.

If you find that you prefer one exercise to another, fine. That is to be expected. However, I recommend that you observe the planned sequence presented and try each exercise in turn, at least a few times, before moving on. Of course, you may also wish to return to a particular exercise after several weeks or months, with new results likely. Be aware that Exercise 13 can induce a general, inner invigoration . . . it can therefore be done with beneficial effects two or three times a day.

Some of the meditative exercises come from especially evocative realms within the age-old Jewish tradition; although none are associated with more advanced kabbalistic practice. Many of us, however, have not developed our image-making capability; thus one exercise or another might prove too powerful or unsettling for you at the moment. In such a case, it is best simply to skip over it and wait a few weeks or longer, until you feel ready.

Writing in your journal and sharing your meditative experiences with a friend are also important means for achieving a harmonious balance through this inward activity. Choose a pace that is comfortable and not too fast. There is nothing to be gained from forcing matters; the heavenly ladder is to be scaled one step at a time.

There may be times when you wish to speed up your progress, because outwardly, little seems to be happening in your life; but it is wise to be diligent and patient in your efforts. However intense your motivation, it would be unrealistic for you to expect to develop a masterful piano technique overnight; similarly, your inner capacities require repeated practice to become truly potent. Nevertheless, you may find that these exercises appear to generate sudden and propitious "coincidences," or an immediate creative flowering in your life. Others have experienced this turn of events, and you may too. In this respect, just remember that the universe is full of surprises, more than our conscious minds can conceive.

### Getting Ready: Relaxation

The exercises below will be most effective if you observe a few simple guidelines. First, you should be reasonably awake and alert; do not try them when you are fatigued, or they may do more harm than good. Second, make yourself as physically comfortable as possible in a seated position; if you lie down, you may drift off to sleep. Take off your shoes, jewelry, and watch; loosen your outer clothing. Make sure you will be undisturbed by any possible intrusion or distraction for at least the next half hour.

Now, close your lips lightly and focus your attention on your breath as it leaves and then returns to your nostrils. Do not alter your breathing pattern. Simply become aware of your breath and how it steadily and evenly flows through you.

As you breathe in, feel the energy you are taking in fill your being with vitality. As you breathe out, feel all the wastes and toxins accumulated throughout your body dissipate. Let your muscles relax in every part of your body, as you become aware of your growing relaxation and calmness. Continue this rhythmic activity for several minutes, until you are relaxed yet alert.

Complete these preliminaries before you begin each exercise.

*Exercise 13.  The Ein Sof* (The Infinite)

After you have completed the preliminary relaxation described above, visualize your inner self soaring upward. As you ascend, you feel a growing sense of lightness and mental clarity. As you soar higher and higher now, you become aware of the dazzling sea of Light that shines all around you.

This Light is the *Ein Sof*; it is filled with boundless, creative strength. At this very moment, and every moment of existence, it is creating the entire universe anew in dazzling, cascading energy.

Feel the radiance of the *Ein Sof* as it fills the cosmos and the countless stars and worlds of space. This Light connects them all into one supreme whole. Feel this radiance flowing through you and invigorating you with a marvelous sense of well-being. Know that whatever creative energy you wish in your daily life—whatever activities you are involved in—this Light is right now generating all the creativity to guide you and help you. Indeed, it is infinite creativity, the source of All.

Gently be aware of this brilliant radiance—flowing throughout the myriad aspects of the cosmos, and through you—for as long as you wish. When you feel ready, let your inner self descend until it merges with your normal being. Take a few moments to rest quietly. Now, go about your day's activities.

*Exercise 14.  The Tree of Life*

Begin with the preliminary relaxation. Then, visualize the following image (taken verbatim from the *Zohar*), saying the words aloud until the picture is vivid and real. At that moment, close your eyes and continue to focus upon this image. You may wish to visualize your inner self soaring upward through dazzling realms of space, and materializing before this radiant scene.

In the beginning, the House of the World was made. This House forms the center of the universe, and it has many doors and entrance chambers on all sides, sacred and exalted abodes where the celestial birds build their nests, each according to its kind.

From the midst of the House, rises a large Tree, with mighty branches and abundance of fruit providing food for all, which rears itself to the clouds of heaven and is lost to view between three rocks, from which the

Tree again emerges, so that it is both above and below them. From this Tree, the House is watered.

In this House are stored may precious and undiscovered treasures. That Tree is visible in the daytime, but hidden at night.

As you gaze at the House of the World and the Tree of Life, feel their wondrous vitality connected to you. Feel their splendor radiating throughout the universe. As you continue to gaze, you feel the same, indestructible energy that reverberates through the House and Tree also cascading through your entire being. You feel refreshed, filled with vitality.

When you are ready, gently depart the scene, as you leave with your visage still facing it. Once more you are in dazzling space. Now, you are back in your room. Feel your inner self merge with your normal being. With the beauty and brilliance of the vision within you, go about your day's activities.

*Exercise 15.   Within the Sacred House*

Complete the relaxation and begin this exercise precisely as you did the previous one. This time, as you stand before the House of ʻie World and the Tree of Life, you see a door in the center of the House. The door is slightly ajar, as if welcoming your presence. Gently push open the door, and enter the House.

As you step in, you see the House is serene and beautiful. The light within it is wondrous, and its radiance fills you with calmness and well-being. In the distance, you can see the massive trunk of the Tree, as it rises into the heavens. Near you, in the room you are standing in, is a treasure chest inlaid with dazzling jewels of every kind.

Know that within the chest is an object, or set of objects, that will guide you creatively with an issue or challenge in your present life. Go over to the treasure chest and open it. What do you see? Feel free to handle or use the object or objects in any way you desire, for as long as you wish.

When you have finished your actions, place the materials gently back in the treasure chest. Now, close the chest, and return outside the House of the World through the door from which you entered. Feel yourself soar through dazzling space and then materialize back in your room at home. Now, feel yourself merge with your normal being. The vitality and benefit from this experience will guide you as you go about your day's activities.

### Exercise 16.   The Cave of Machpelah*

Carry out your usual preliminaries. This time, your inner self soars upward and materializes in the Land of Israel. You are in the countryside in the time of Abraham. Before you is a cave in the hills, the holy Cave of Machpelah.

You enter the Cave and feel its cool, moist air. You become aware of your growing sense of mental clarity and inner refreshment. As you look about the Cave, you see a door in the rear wall. You open the glowing door and step through it. Before you lies the Garden of Eden.

You behold its lush splendor shimmering in a heavenly light. Its radiance fills you with joy and delight; it stretches in every direction to the horizon.

As you stand in the Garden of Eden, you feel its exalted brilliance shining all around you. From within the lush vegetation, a gentle and wise animal comes toward you. It knows you well. It has an important and helpful message to give you, a message to guide you in your present life—perhaps, relating to an issue you are aware of, or one that has not yet crossed your conscious mind. Wordlessly, the animal gazes at you with understanding and communicates its message through its eyes to yours. This process may happen instantaneously, or it may take several minutes or longer.

What is this message? You may with to say it aloud so that you will better remember it. Now, express your gratitude to the creature for its guidance; watch it depart back on its path.

When you have done so, return back through the door into the Cave of Machpelah. Once again, feel its cool, moist air. As you step out of the cave, feel your inner self soar upward from the Land of Israel in the time of Abraham and return to your present room. Merge with your normal being. Know that this experience will aid you as you go about your day's activities.

---

*According to ancient Jewish tradition, the Cave of Machpelah is the burial site of Abraham and Sarah. It has long been imbued with mystical properties and is deemed the entranceway to the Garden of Eden.

*Exercise 17.  Three Doors*

Complete the relaxation. Once again, your inner self flies upward and materializes in the Land of Israel, by the sacred Cave of Machpelah. It is the time of Abraham. You enter the Cave and feel its moist, cool air invigorate and refresh you.

As you look about the Cave, you see three doors in the recesses of the rear wall: one door on your left, one in the center, and one on your right. Step to the door on your left. When you open it, you will see a scene from your past—one that has special meaning and relevance to your present life. This scene will help you to better understand and effectively deal with a current issue of concern or a new challenge.

Now, open the door and enter the scene. What do you see? Stay in the surroundings for as long as you wish. When you have sufficiently observed the scene in all its details, step back into the Cave of Machpelah. The air is cool and refreshing once more.

Now, advance toward the center door. It will open onto a scene revealing something that is happening at present in your life. Open the door and step in. What do you see? When you have observed the scene in all its details, return to the Cave of Machpelah.

Now, walk toward the door on your right. It will open onto a scene from your possible future, something you would inwardly like to have happen very much. The scene may be several months or even several years ahead. Open the door and enter this scene. What do you see?

When you have finished observing this scene in all its details, step back into the Cave of Machpelah. As you feel its cool, moist air on your body, know that each of these experiences has given you added strength and energy in your daily life—and greater insight into your current situation.

Now, walk out of the Cave of Machpelah into the countryside of Israel in the time of Abraham. Your inner self flies upward and returns to your room. It merges with your normal being. You may wish to record your three experiences in your journal. With a sense of renewed vitality, go about your day's activities.

110 / SPIRITUAL EXERCISES

*Exercise 18. The Flying Scroll\**

Carry out your usual preliminaries, placing your journal and a writing instrument close beside you. This time, feel your inner self soar upward and materialize in the Land of Israel. It is nearly two thousand years ago. The holy Temple of Jerusalem no longer exists on earth, but its rays of glory bathe the landscape around you in a shimmering beauty. A sense of lightness and serenity fills your being.

As you walk along in warm sunlight, you see a flying scroll materialize and stop near you in mid-air. It appears to have radiant wings on either side as it hovers closer. The scroll is now right in front of you.

Gazing steadily at the scroll, you begin to see clearly its message. It has been sent from above to help you with a present issue in your life or perhaps a new challenge. The message may be long or short; it may also have pictures or images. But whatever form the message takes, its meaning is both timely and quite beneficial to you.

What does the message say? If you wish, copy the message of the scroll onto your journal. Keep your eyes still half-closed as you do so.

When you have finished writing, feel the scroll slowly lift upward and then steadily ascend until it disappears. With a buoyant awareness of purpose and clarity, feel your inner self soar upward and return to your room. It merges with your normal being. Feel your connection to your higher Source of wisdom, as you go about your day's activities.

*Exercise 19. Revelation†*

Carry out your usual preliminaries. This time, feel your inner self fly upward and materialize in the Land of Israel. It is the time of Moses and the great Exodus of the Jews from Egypt. You stand on a plain before the holy Mount Sinai, with all the Jewish souls

---

*The theme of the divine scroll figures prominently in Judaism; this image appears in the Book of Ezekiel, the *Zohar*, and other visionary works.

†Jewish tradition affirms that every Jewish soul was present when the Ten Commandments were given—that indeed, all humanity heard God at that holy moment. The Kabbalah teaches that the Divine Voice continues to issue forth from Mount Sinai, but that we no longer perceive it.

around you who have ever lived. You are about to receive the divine Revelation now.

From the mountaintop ringed with clouds emanates the dazzling radiance of the Creator, brighter than a thousand suns. As you stand, you become aware that your body is completely translucent and is radiating light like a living star of wondrous energy and vitality. You are filled with a sense of unexpressible well-being.

In this sacred moment within Eternity, you begin to hear a barely audible, wordless hum or melody sung by every soul of the Jewish people. This song, growing in strength and intensity, permeates your heart with great happiness and vibrancy, and reverberates from one end of the universe to the other. You may wish to hum or sing aloud this melody within you.

Let your body sway or move in any way that you desire. Let yourself express, as freely as you can, whatever emotion wells inside you.

When you feel ready and invigorated with a new sense of purpose and energy, feel your inner self soar upward from the Land of Israel in the time of Moses. Feel your inner self return to your room and merge with your normal being. If you wish, you may record what you have just experienced. Now, slowly rise and go about your day's activities.

*Exercise 20.   Welcoming Elijah*

Conduct your usual preliminaries, making yourself as comfortable as possible. The moment has now come for Elijah to enter your life in a direct way. Through the passage of the years, he has been aware, of course, of your own emotional and spiritual growth—your joys and frustrations. At this time, you have been found worthy of a special visit from him, on his appointed rounds to every land of the globe.

As you close your eyes, be aware that Elijah's presence is drawing near. The more receptive and intent you are to receive his message, the greater will be the communion between you. Throughout the centuries, Jewish sages have taught that Elijah always travels in disguise; as an ascended prophet, he has no earthly form whatever, but takes on the visual characteristics and attire suitable for his encounter with each man or woman. Thus Elijah will come to you and appear in a manner you will personally find most beneficial and comforting.

With your eyes closed, now feel Elijah's presence almost within your room. In your mind's eye, see him enter and stand near you, as you wordlessly greet him. Making yourself as receptive as possible, listen to his message. It may be short or long—general or quite specific—but its content intimately relates to your emotional and spiritual development. His message may pertain to your attitudes and traits, habitual conduct, or plans. In any event, it encompasses your future as well, for he sees beyond the daily, mundane matters of your life.

When Elijah has completed his message to you, express your gratitude and feel his holy presence depart from your room. Know that he remains vitally interested in your growth toward the divine. Now, gently open your eyes. You may wish to record Elijah's message in your journal. Go about your day's activities, and feel refreshed with renewed strength.

### Exercise 21. The Heavenly Ladder

Carry out your usual preliminaries. Feel your inner self fly upward and materialize in the Land of Israel. It is the time of Jacob— Isaac's son—in the ancient past. The countryside is luminous with celestial light, as night begins to fall. The wide bowl of sky is soon filled with dazzling stars. You stand on the sacred ground which will later become the site of the First and Second Temple of Jerusalem. Feel yourself gently lie down now on the soft earth. Taking one of the stones you see, place it under your head as a pillow. Gaze up at the night sky, brilliant with myriad pinpoints of light. Gradually, you notice that a shimmering Ladder is forming before you—its base rests solidly on the ground and its pinnacle disappears into the distance above you.

When you are ready, feel yourself get up and begin to climb the Ladder. With the speed of thought, you have ascended each rung in turn and have passed through many layers of clouds. As you climb through the last cloud-barrier, you now enter a scene that has personal meaning for you. This is a higher realm—one situated above mundane existence—and the scene has special relevance for an issue or challenge you are facing in your present life.

Experience this scene for as long as you wish. It may involve people or events from your past, current circumstances, or possible future. But it possesses particular importance for your inner wholeness. Know that you can return to this scene at any time for further understanding.

When you have sufficiently absorbed the meaning of this visual realm, feel yourself descend the Ladder. Once more, you are moving through layers of clouds and back to earth. With the speed of thought, you have come down each rung. As you step onto the ground, you feel vibrant and invigorated. A few instants later, the Ladder begins to lose its form and vanishes. Dawn has started to break over the Land of Israel.

Let your inner self fly upward and materialize back in your room. It merges with your normal being. Go about your day's activities, as your inward ascent will give you renewed purpose and inner direction.

### Exercise 22.  The Heavenly Tribunal

One of Judaism's most beautiful and powerful concepts is that of the Heavenly Tribunal. In written form, this theme dates back to the biblical Book of Daniel, if not earlier. For millennia, Jewish sages have taught that when each soul departs from earthly existence, it is summoned to appear before the celestial court of justice. And in that summoning, each soul must review and account for every deed, every word, and even every thought that it generated during its abode on earth.

The kabbalistic and later Hasidic tradition have had much to say on this provocative subject. Mystical adepts have emphasized that each of our acts, words, and thoughts leaves an indelible mark on the universe; nothing stands in true isolation from the divine whole. Thus the *Zohar* succinctly states that, "If a person does kindness on earth, he awakens loving-kindness above, and it rests upon that day which is crowned therewith through him. Similarly, if he performs a deed of mercy, he crowns that day with mercy and it becomes his protector in the hour of need."

Conduct your usual preliminaries, making sure you are in a receptive and alert mood. You are about to go on a vital mission— to the exalted chamber of the Heavenly Tribunal. You are volunteering to review your life now as a way to carry out more forcefully and joyfully your soul's particular purpose on earth. The Heavenly Tribunal, of course, is aware of your intent and approves; because of your honesty and openness, it will provide the guidance you need.

When you feel ready, let your inner self soar upward, upward into the far reaches of the divine worlds that everywhere exist. You are now before the celestial Court. Choose a particular period of time—for example, the past week, month or year. Or, you may wish to focus on an especially important period of your distant past, perhaps an episode never fully clarified or resolved within you. Feeling the emotional support of the divine Court, begin to dispassionately examine your actions, words to others, and dominant thoughts.

If you find an incident when your Higher Self or *neshamah* shone, be grateful and fix it in your memory. If you encounter an episode when a lower impulse triumphed, now visualize yourself in that same time—behaving, speaking, or thinking in a beneficial manner. For as Rabbi Nachman of Bratslav poetically observed, ''If a person does not judge himself, all things judge him, and all things become messengers of God.''

When you have completed your self-examination, ask the Heavenly Tribunal for guidance in leading you toward a more harmonious life. You may wish to close your eyes and silently absorb the response of the Court. Finally, thank the Holy One for allowing the blessing of what you have just experienced.

Feel your inner self returning from the higher worlds, back to this earthly realm. Merge with your normal being. You may wish to record this encounter in your journal. Be aware that the Heavenly Tribunal stands ready to assist you again, whenever you seek its wisdom. Go about your day's activities with renewed strength and purpose.

### Exercise 23. The Book of Raziel

Carry out your usual preliminaries; keep your journal close at hand. This time, feel your inner self soar upward and materialize in the Land of Israel. It is almost two thousand years ago. The holy Temple of Jerusalem has departed from the earth, but its celestial rays fill the landscape around you in a dazzling beauty. Everything seems luminous as you see a cave in the hills before you.

Feel yourself walking lightly and evenly toward the cave. With each step you take, you experience a heightened sense of well-being and vitality. As you reach the cave and enter it, you feel its cool, moist air. Take a few breaths. After some moments, you notice in the dim light a special plot of earth at the center of the cave. Advancing toward the patch of earth, you see that an old manuscript lies almost hidden from view.

Dust off the manuscript and take it into your hands. It is the sacred Book of Raziel—shared by the angels with Adam, Noah, and other holy figures—to help teach them the secrets of the universe. All knowledge is contained within the Book Raziel. Know that it has become available to you now, to provide guidance on a particular issue or challenge in your present life.

Open the Book of Raziel and turn to the first page that feels right. There is a divine message for you. As you gaze at the page, its content begins to be clear. The message may be short or long; it may comprise just a few key words, or perhaps several sentences or even paragraphs. Pictures or images may be visible too. Whatever the nature of the message, its meaning is timely and valuable to you.

What does the message say? If you wish, copy the message in the Book of Raziel onto your journal. Keep your eyes still half-closed as you do so.

When you have finished writing, let your inner self close the Book of Raziel and return it to its place in the cave. With a sense of renewed purpose and clarity, depart from the cave. Once outside, continue back along your same path in the countryside of Israel. Feel your inner self soar upward and return to your room. Merge with your normal being. With this holy wisdom to inspire you, now go about your day's activities.

*Exercise 24.   The Heavenly Academy*

For many centuries, the Jewish visionary tradition has emphasized the notion of the Heavenly Academy. According to this evocative conception, the greatest sages of all humanity inhabit this lofty realm of paradise. There, in a state of existence transcendent of time and space—and imbued with a radiance beyond our comprehension—they continue to explore the innermost secrets of the Torah, and consequently, the deepest mysteries of the universe.

In this celestial abode, we are told, such dazzling souls as Abraham and Seth, Elijah and Isaiah, Moses and Rabbi Akiba, King David and Hillel the Elder, and, more recently, Rabbi Isaac Luria and the Baal Shem Tov, converse in the closest harmony of intellect and emotion. Many other pious souls, obscured by the vagaries of history, also reside there. Liberated from earthly constraints, together all dwell in ecstasy as they further their knowledge of the "worlds upon worlds" that comprise the divine order.

Conduct your usual preliminaries, and make yourself relaxed and comfortable. You are to embark on an important and exciting journey—to the abode of the Heavenly Academy. Your mission? To receive the sages' guidance on how you can best grow now in wisdom and discernment. With their supernal qualities, the sages are aware of your coming and your sincere aspirations for higher development. Indeed, they know you quite well and welcome your visit.

You will be permitted to ask three questions of the Heavenly Academy. Each question will relate to your present life; their responses will help guide and strengthen your sense of personal direction. You may wish to visualize a specific figure who will meet with you—say, Abraham or the Baal Shem Tov, though of course those in the Heavenly Academy have no real bodily form.

When you feel ready, let your inner self soar upward, upward, until you are at the abode of the Heavenly Academy. Now, offer your first question: What specific knowledge do I need to acquire in my current circumstances? The sages may wish to direct you to read certain books, study certain material, or, in a less intellectual way, gain certain insights about life that you do not yet possess. The response of the Heavenly Academy may be reassuring or rather surprising.

Now, ask your second question: How am I to acquire this knowledge? The sages may direct you to a special person or group, or to a definite field of study or performance. Their advice may be more general, and they may simply point you toward a certain path that requires your exploration.

Now, you are ready to present your third and final question: What aspects of my current knowledge and talents am I not expressing properly or allowing to lie unused? For the sages have always considered it vital that we fully actualize all that we are and all that we can be. They may point your attention to matters that you have recognized for some time—or they may bring your awareness to attributes you have scarcely thought of.

Now, offer your gratitude to the Heavenly Academy for its guidance. When you have done so, feel your inner self descend steadily and harmoniously to your room. Merge with your normal being. You may wish to record in your journal the specific advice of the Heavenly Tribunal. Afterward, go about your day's activities as you feel revitalized and renewed.

For this exercise and all the others, remember the inspiring advice of the Midrash: ''The gates are open at every hour, and all who wish to enter, may enter.''

# 7

# THE ALPHABET OF CREATION

Judaism has always regarded Hebrew as a sacred language, the medium of divine communication. Throughout the major Jewish texts, down the centuries, the sages have taught that the letters are no ordinary vehicle of expression. Rather, as the Talmud, Midrash, and many kabbalistic works insist, the Hebrew alphabet bears a host of hidden significances. The more we learn about the letters—through both study and meditation—we are told, the greater becomes our own inner strength and discernment.

In traditional Jewish thought, each letter—its name, pictorial form, numerical equivalent, and respective position in the alphabet—is ordained by the Holy One. As corollary of this principle, Jewish law has for millennia decreed that every letter of a Torah scroll must be perfect, or else the entire scroll is forbidden to be used. Not a fragment of a single letter may be omitted or distorted; nor may its individual character be compromised by contact with any other letters. Every word must be spelled correctly; one extra, transposed, or missing letter invalidates the whole scroll.

This religious dictum itself can be seen to impart a higher lesson: each person, like each letter in the Torah, has a unique purpose in the divine plan. No one may infringe on another's particular mission in life, just as no two letters may overlap.

The classic sources relate that the Hebrew alphabet contains the secrets of the universe. For example, in speaking of the master builder of the holy Tabernacle in the Wilderness, the Talmud comments that, "Bezalel knew how to combine the letters with which heaven and earth were created." The scholars went on to compare such recondite wisdom to that with which God created the cosmos.

In a more detailed passage, the Talmud provides a brief but complete introductory lesson on the special import of every Hebrew letter.

From the earliest metaphysical text, the *Sefer Yetzirah,* Jewish mystics have extolled the Hebrew alphabet as the manifestation of celestial patterns of energy. In a section that has long entranced kabbalistic adepts, this ancient treatise vividly declares, "Twenty-two foundation letters: He ordained them, He hewed them, He combined them, He weighed them, He interchanged them. And He created with them the whole creation and everything to be created in the future."

Based on this provocative notion, later Jewish visionaries stressed that mastery of the Hebrew alphabet—in all its manifold aspects—allows the individual to gain actual control over the realm of matter. In particular, they regarded the Names of God as powerful devices in the hands of the knowledgeable. The correct permutation and pronunciation of certain Divine Names was believed to grant humans the ability to cure the dangerously ill, perceive events far away in space and time, and even to create a *golem.* Indeed, according to Midrashic legends that flourished about King Solomon of the Bible, he possessed a ring inscribed with a particular Name of God. This ring, it is said, enabled Solomon to carry out uncanny feats of power and wisdom.

Other Jewish legends relate that the Hebrew alphabet exists independently of ink and paper, and even words. The Midrash indicates that before the creation of the universe was completed, God determined the precise shape and serial position of every letter; each vied with all the rest for the honor of being the first to begin the sacred order. We are told that when Moses shattered the first set of tablets, the letters ascended back to the Holy One who gave them.

The *Zohar* is filled with references to the importance of the Hebrew alphabet as a celestial code that embodies the very nature of the cosmos. Modern science, interestingly, can supply an analogy to clarify this evocative concept. That is, just as we now regard the DNA molecule as a carrier of incredibly condensed information concerning the development of life, so too have kabbalists viewed the Hebrew language of Scripture as a cipher describing the universe.

The *Zohar* affirms that every sentence, every phrase, every word, and every letter of the Bible exists simultaneously on several levels of meaning. Thus, this sacred work clearly declares, "Woe unto those who see in the Law nothing but simple narratives and ordinary words! . . . . Every word of the Law contains an elevated sense and a sublime mystery."

In keeping with this notion, the *Zohar* devotes an entire section to the subtleties reflected in the single word *Bereshith* (usually translated as simply "In the Beginning"), which opens the Book of Genesis and the Bible. Moreover, there is even a detailed discussion on the single letter *Bet,* which begins that first word. This approach to Scripture—and the Hebrew language that communicates it—has remained fundamental to the Kabbalah.

Abraham ben Samuel Abulafia (c. 1240–1292) was one of the most important Jewish mystics, due to his development of a system of meditation based on the Hebrew alphabet. Influenced by Maimonides's ideas—that each of us has the potential to attain heightened states of consciousness, even those associated with divine prophecy—Abulafia taught in a practical way that the Hebrew letters are a key pathway to the Holy Source within. He emphasized that through proper understanding and practice, any person can use the Hebrew language as a means to arouse tremendous, intuitive capabilities. "Look at these holy letters with truth and belief," he advised, "[it] will awaken the heart to thoughts of godly and prophetic images."

Abulafia preached that the path to higher awareness is not a particularly difficult one. He recommended that initiates keep themselves in vibrant physical health, for like Maimonides, he believed that we are cloaked in divine coverings of matter—and that the human body is a sacred vessel. Indeed, Abulafia's yoga-like exercises involving altered modes of breathing require strong bodily vitality, or else harm may result.

The crucial aspect of Abulafia's system is the utilization of the Hebrew language as the vehicle by which one ascends into the transcendent world. He referred to this process as "knowing God through the method of the twenty-two letters of the alphabet." In specific advice to his disciples, Abulafia stated, "Cleanse your body, and choose a special place where none will hear you, and remain altogether by yourself in isolation. Sit in one place in a room, or in the attic . . . it is best to do it by night."

In Abulafia's approach, then, the individual "begins to combine letters, a few or many, reversing and rolling them around rapidly, until [one's] heart feels warm.'' If a person adheres diligently to this technique, Abulafia declared, he will eventually experience ''a plenitude of saintly spirit . . . wisdom, understanding, good counsel and knowledge . . . The spirit of the Lord will rest upon him.''

Because Abulafia was a lay kabbalist and strongly advocated an unconventional, individualist orientation to self-transformation, he experienced much antagonism from the rabbinical establishment of his day. But he inspired small groups of followers throughout the Mediterranean region. Down to the present day, Abulafia's creative means for awakening intuition are practiced by people around the globe.

In the centuries that have passed since Abulafia promulgated his intriguing approach to meditation, many Jewish thinkers have stressed the power of the Hebrew letters when we concentrate on them with the proper will or *kavvanah*. In the sixteenth century, the renowned Rabbi Isaac Luria, the Ari, introduced a variety of meditative methods, but viewed the Hebrew language as possessing a divine force of its own.

Legend has it that once, during the Days of Awe, the Ari felt that his prayers were particularly effective. But the Almighty suddenly revealed to him that another's prayers were even more potent that his. Quite intrigued, Rabbi Luria sought out and found the man, who seemed a most ordinary villager.

''What did you do during the Days of Awe?'' Rabbi Luria asked.

The man replied that he was unlearned and could not even read the entire Hebrew alphabet. So, when the services began at his synagogue, he recited the first ten letters and said, ''Please, O Master of the Universe, take my letters and form them into words that will please You.'' And he repeated this phrase all day long.

Upon hearing the simple man's account, Rabbi Luria then understood that the heartfelt prayers of the ignorant villager had been more exalted than all others.

The early Hasidic leaders likewise venerated the Hebrew letters as vessels of the divine. The Baal Shem Tov placed great emphasis on this notion, both through colorful parables to the unschooled folk and high complex kabbalistic teachings to selected disciples. ''Every physical thing contains these twenty-two letters,'' he commented, ''with which the world and everything in it are revealed.'' On another occasion, the Besht is attributed to have observed that,

"All things were created through combinations of the twenty-two letters."

There are many Hasidic tales that point to the holiness inherent in the Hebrew alphabet. According to one legend, a terrible decree against the Jews was once issued in heaven. The Besht summoned two of his close companions and together sought to find a means to nullify this sentence of the Heavenly Tribunal. In deep meditation, the Hasidic founder learned that the decree was beyond repeal; yet, at the same time, he became aware that someone's words and thoughts were causing a dazzling light to fill the supernal regions.

Deciding to pursue this matter, the Baal Shem Tov traveled through the higher realms and located the radiant source. It was a humble villager who was accustomed to recite the whole Book of Psalms five times each day. The letters were creating the brilliant glow cascading through the universe.

Returning to earthly form, the Hasidic founder visited the man and asked him, "If you knew that your portion in the World to Come could be used to save a Jewish village, would you relinquish it?"

"If I actually have a portion in the World to Come," the man responded simply, "I would be glad to give it away to save a Jewish settlement."

At that moment, the heavenly decree was abolished.

In another Hasidic story, an ignorant but pious Jewish farmer was journeying to a nearby village, to attend synagogue services for Yom Kippur. Unfortunately, he lost his way in the forest. As the daylight dwindled, the man realized to his dismay that Yom Kippur eve, the holiest time of the year, had come.

Not having a prayerbook and not knowing the prayers by heart, the forlorn farmer cried out to the Almighty, "Master of the Universe, what can I do? How can I pray to you? I will recite the Hebrew alphabet and You, You put the letters together to make the right words." And he repeated the letters over and over, until he felt the peace within.

This unlearned man's prayers, it is said, were more potent than those of far more erudite figures.

## Going Inward

The meditative exercises to follow are based on the ideas mentioned earlier in this chapter—that the Hebrew language is a valuable tool for self-advancement. They are designed to help develop your ability to focus your attention and enhance your creative potential.

I recommended that, consistent with time-honored Jewish practice, you conduct these sessions at night, in a quiet room lit only by candles. The light should be bright enough to enable you to see clearly. As Abraham Abulafia advised his ardent disciples more than a half-millennia ago, "Take in hand pen and ink and a writing board, and this will be your witness that you have come to serve your God with joy and with gladness of heart."

Twenty to thirty minutes per session is quite adequate when you are starting out; you may wish to gradually increase the amount of time as you become more proficient in your efforts. Through many sessions with both groups and individuals, I have found that men and women typically develop mental associations with the letters that are amazingly consistent with age-old Jewish esoteric writings. Many also report quite spontaneous and uplifting spiritual experiences as a result of such meditations. These phenomena have certainly convinced me that the Hebrew letters are indeed primal or archetypal forces within our deep consciousness, just as the kabbalists have for many centuries insisted. Who knows what else we will soon find confirmed in the visionary tradition? Let us begin to find out.

Get yourself a large sketch pad (at least 8 inches by 11 inches) or sheaf of white, unlined paper. A drawing pen with black ink will be helpful, though other writing utensils are also effective. Carry out your usual preliminaries to quiet your mind; keep your journal close by.

Now, copy each of the letters of the Hebrew alphabet in order, as you see them on page 124. Take your time with each letter and do not skip any. As you draw the letters, each should have plenty of space around it.

During your copying, be aware that each letter is both a symbol and a pictorial representation of a particular cosmic—and human—situation. For example, the first letter, *Aleph,* is characteristically

*Exercise 25.* *Introduction to the Letters*

### THE ALPHABET OF CREATION

| | | | | | | |
|---|---|---|---|---|---|---|
| א | ALEPH | 1 | | ס | SAMECH | 60 |
| ב | BETH | 2 | | ע | AYIN | 70 |
| ב | VETH | 2 | | פ | PAY | 80 |
| ג | GIMEL | 3 | | פ | PHAY | 80 |
| ד | DALETH | 4 | | צ | TZADDE | 90 |
| ה | HAY | 5 | | ק | KUPH | 100 |
| ו | VAV | 6 | | ר | RESH | 200 |
| ז | ZAYIN | 7 | | ש | SHIN | 300 |
| ח | CHETH | 8 | | ש | SIN | 300 |
| ט | TETH | 9 | | ת | TAV | 400 |
| י | YOD | 10 | | ת | THAV | 400 |
| כ | CAPH | 20 | | ך | FINAL CHAPH | 500 |
| כ | CHAPH | 20 | | ם | FINAL MEM | 600 |
| ל | LAMED | 30 | | ן | FINAL NUN | 700 |
| מ | MEM | 40 | | ף | FINAL PHAY | 800 |
| נ | NUN | 50 | | ץ | FINAL TZADDE | 900 |

seen as a glyph of an individual with arms outstretched in action; this letter also symbolically stands for the primordial generative energy of the universe. The second letter, *Beth,* has been viewed as a pictorial representation of a house, and a symbol of the universal "feminine" or nurturing force.

Let your imagination soar as you intuitively sense the statement that each letter makes to you. Remember Abraham Abulafia's poetic suggestion to concentrate "on all of them, in all their aspects, like a person who is told a parable, or a riddle, or a dream, or as one who ponders a book of wisdom in a subject so profound . . . . " Note whether you feel a special affinity for any specific letters, for this relationship is significant, too.

You may copy the entire Hebrew alphabet two or three times in any one session. But after each sequence, pause for a few minutes to observe any images, thoughts, or feelings that may have arisen in your mind. At the end of the session, record in your journal what you have experienced.

### Exercise 26.  Forces of Power

Carry out your usual preliminaries; you will need the same materials as for the previous exercise. This time, select four letters of the Hebrew alphabet that you find especially appealing and provocative. The number four has many esoteric associations; kabbalists, for example, have long preached that four separate but interrelated realms exist in the cosmos. These range from the radiant dimension of the *Ein Sof,* beyond all space and time, down to our own, everyday world of matter.

Devote several minutes now to drawing the first of these letters in various ways. As long as the shape is recognizable, you may be as inventive, fanciful, or stylistic as you choose.

After you have filled your pages with many illustrations of the first letter you have selected, pause and be aware of any impressions that may have appeared in your mind. Record these reactions in your journal. Then continue in the same manner with the next three letters, likewise pausing after each one to note your personal responses.

As you carry out this exercise, you may notice that certain specific letters exert particular effects upon you—for example, one letter may induce a feeling of deep calmness, while another may awaken the impulse for energetic activity. Be aware of such results, for they are quite consistent with longstanding Jewish thought concerning the Hebrew alphabet.

You may also discover that some letters evoke an immediate effect on your state of mind, whereas others seem to have little or no impact at all. This situation, too, is worth nothing. Those letters you find most appealing are probably representative of personality traits that are salient within you; on the other hand, those letters which appear to leave you cold, are most likely representative of inner faculties that lie dormant.

Over a period of days or weeks, you may therefore wish to focus on each letter of the Hebrew alphabet. For just as all twenty-two letters are said to be harmoniously integrated as part of the divine plan of Creation, all of our characteristics within need to be balanced and arrayed appropriately. Ultimately, every Hebrew letter will spark for you a heightened perception of the world and its splendor.

### Exercise 27. Living Letters

Carry out your usual preliminaries. Once more, chose four letters of the Hebrew alphabet on which to focus your attention. Concentrate on the first letter until it is clear and vivid in your mind's eye—until you can see its lucid form even with your eyes closed. The Midrash tells us that God gave the Torah to Moses as black fire superimposed on white fire; you may find this image helpful as you concentrate on each letter.

Now, feel your inner self soar upward and materialize in the Land of Israel. It is the time of the glory of the holy Temple of Jerusalem. You stand on a plain bathed in its golden and serene rays. You feel calm and filled with well-being.

Before you on the earth, vast and radiant with glowing energy, stands that same Hebrew letter. It now towers many stories high over the landscape; its top rises far into the sky, its height is so great.

Explore the three-dimensional structure of the Hebrew letter as fully as possible. Since you are light and weightless, fly about, observing and feeling the letter's vibrant form. As you do so, feel the divine, living power that animates it. For, as the Jewish mystical tradition teaches, Creation is occurring at every moment anew, sustaining the universe and everything within it. Feel this power imbuing you with creative strength.

When you have sufficiently explored the first letter you have chosen, let your inner self fly upward, return to your room, and merge with your normal being. After a pause, record in your journal whatever thoughts, feelings, or ideas you may have had. Continue in this manner with each of the three other Hebrew letters you have selected. As with the previous exercise, you may wish to carry out this one too with every letter of the alphabet—over a period of several weeks. This method will further strengthen the divine aspects within you to which the sacred vessels of communication correspond.

### Exercise 28. Night Sky

Carry out your usual preliminaries. Now, visualize your inner self fly upward and materialize in the Land of Israel. It is a lovely, serene night at the time of the splendor of the Temple of Jerusalem. You gaze up at the dark, black sky filled with thousands of glowing stars. Indeed, the vast heavens above you seem overglowing with points of holy Light.

As you look upward and feel a wondrous sense of peace and joy, the points of light begin to shift and move. You see that they have formed a giant Hebrew letter in the sky, like a great constellation. For the *Zohar* teaches that the Hebrew letters form shapes in the sky and divine messages thereby come to us. Continue to gaze at the letter, feeling its divine energy cascading throughout the universe and flowing through you.

When you have sufficiently absorbed this celestial energy, see the letter fade and disappear. And now, a second Hebrew letter appears, until the heavens are lit up by its brightness too. When the power of this energy has invigorated you, the letter begins to fade and then vanish. And thereupon, a third Hebrew letter emerges out of the blackness and amidst the countless points of light in the sky. Like a great constellation, this letter also fills the heavens. When its brilliance has permeated your own form with its pulsating vitality, you see it fade and vanish.

Now, a fourth Hebrew letter beings to take shape and splendor over in the starry skies over the Land of Israel. When you have absorbed its exalted glow, this last Hebrew letter fades and disappears. Feel the serene night air around you for a few minutes of deep stillness.

Your inner self flies upward, materializes back in your room, and merges with your normal being. Now, record in your journal any particular ideas of feelings that arose during the course of this exercise.

Beginners may decide to carry out this method with each Hebrew letter in its alphabetical order. The next step is to allow the various letters to come forth spontaneously, as just described.

If you are more advanced and proficient in Hebrew, you may choose to meditate upon the word or words that emerge in this exercise. You may also wish to make use of the kabbalistic technique of *Notarikon,* in which words are broken down into individual letters, each of which then becomes the initial of another word. Thus a four-word sentence with personal meaning for you can be generated from the four letters that appear in each session.

In any event, the Hebrew language has inspired individuals for thousands of years. Its letters have long been venerated as emanations from the Holy One and deemed worthy of our close attention. By devoting time and concentration to them, we can greatly benefit within. As Rabbi Nachman of Bratslav recommended, "You should constantly center your thoughts on contemplating the root of all things. This is the source of all joy."

# GLOSSARY

**Aggadah** The non-legal material in the Talmud, primarily of a legendary character.

**Amora** (pl. **amoraim**) Literally, "speakers" or "interpreters." The name given to the sages who interpreted the Mishnah and related Jewish law in the third through fifth centuries C.E.

**Baal Shem Tov** "Master of the Good Name," the popular appellation of Israel ben Eliezer (c. 1698–1760), the charismatic Hasidic founder.

**Bahir** The mystical *Book of Brilliance,* anonymously written, which first appeared in Provence, southern France, about the year 1175.

**Besht** An abbreviation of the Hebrew name Baal Shem Tov.

**Book of Raziel** A legendary book given by the angel Raziel to Adam at divine command, in which he learned secrets of the universe.

**Ein Sof** The "Infinite," from which all forms in the cosmos are created.

**Galut** Literally, "exile." The forced exile of the Jewish people since the destruction of the Second Temple of Jerusalem, also, the Diaspora.

**Gaon** (pl. **gaonim**) The title associated with the heads of the two outstanding academies in Babylonia, following the close of the Talmud.

**Gemara** (Aramaic) Literally, "to study." It is the commentary surrounding the Mishnah. The Gemara and Mishnah together comprise the Talmud.

**Golem** Literally, "Shapeless mass." According to the Talmud and other works, humans can create such a creature of clay by using mystical techniques.

**Halakha** Literally, "the way to walk." The legal system of Orthodox Judaism.

**Hasidism** The popular, charismatic movement that arose among East European Jewry in the late eighteenth century. *Hasid* means "pious" in Hebrew; in twelfth-century Germany, an unrelated group was likewise known as the *Hasidim.*

**Hirhurey d'yoma** Daydream.

**Hitbodehut** Literally, "self-isolation." The practice of being alone with the deity. Some form of meditation or private devotion is characteristically involved.

**Kabbalah** From the Hebrew root-word "to receive." Often used as a generic term for Jewish mysticism per se, it more precisely refers to esoteric thought from the late twelfth century onward.

**Kavvanah** The classic rabbinical term for mental concentration. Among the Hasidim, *kavvanah* came to be associated with the type of "one-pointedness" of intent necessary for higher states of awareness.

**Lamed-vov** Literally, "thirty-six." According to the Talmud and other works, there are always thirty-six hidden Just Men in every generation, whose combined presence sustains the world.

**Ma'aseh Bereshith** "The Act of Creation." The mystical, conceptual teachings concerning the secrets of Creation.

**Ma'aseh Merkabah** "The Act of the Divine Chariot." The mystical, experiential teachings associated with the biblical vision of Ezekiel.

**Mensch** (Yiddish) Literally, "a person," one who embodies maturity and inner depth.

**Mezzuzah** (pl. *mezzuzos*) Literally, "doorpost." A small case containing a piece of parchment upon which is written the prayer that begins *Shema Yisrael*. This case is affixed to each right doorpost in a Jew's home, in accordance with the biblical injunction.

**Midrash** The legendary tradition of Judaism. A *midrash* (lowercased, with the plural *midrashim*) is a specific Midrashic legend.

**Mishnah** The earliest, post-biblical text of Jewish law and belief. It consists of six orders, each divided into tractates. It is believed to have been completed in the early third century C.E.

**Mittnagedim** Orthodox Jews who were "Opponents" of the Hasidic movement. The *Mittnagedim* went to great lengths to attempt to suppress the spread of Hasidism among East European Jewry.

**Moreh Derekh** "Teacher of the Way." One who instructs in the divine path.

**Musar** Literally, "ethics." The *musar* movement arose among the non-Hasidic Orthodox Jews of Lithuania in the mid-nineteenth century and stressed individual self-improvement.

**Nefesh** The lowest, most physical portion of the human Self. The *nefesh* dissolves upon physical mortality.

**Neshamah** In Jewish tradition, the nonphysical and transcendent part of the Self; it is said to continue after bodily death. Some Jewish mystics suggest that two other, still more immaterial components exist within each of us.

**Notarikon** Meditational technique that breaks Hebrew words into sentences composed of initial letters to attain esoteric knowledge.

**Pirkey Avoth** *The Ethics of the Fathers* The most popular tractate of the Mishnah. It is a collection of aphorisms, governing ethics and conduct, attributed to Jewish sages who lived before the end of the second century C.E.

**Rabbi** Literally, "my teacher." Originally a title for addressing a sage or scholar, it now refers to an individual ordained according to Jewish law.

**Rebbe** Hasidic term for spiritual teacher.

**Ruach** In Jewish tradition, that portion of the human Self intermediate in nature between the *nefesh* and *neshamah*. The *ruach* is said to dissipate shortly after bodily death.

**Ruach Ha-Kadosh** Literally, "the Holy Spirit." It refers to the divine quality felt to illumine the inner life of the holy individual.

**Savoraim** Literally, "expositors." These sages continued to edit the Talmud after its completion; they lived between the late fifth and early seventh centuries.

**Sefer Yetzirah** "Book of Creation," anonymously written between the third and sixth centuries C.E. It represents the earliest metaphysical text in the Hebrew language.

**Sefirot** The ten energy-essences that are said to be in constant interplay and underlie all of the cosmos. The *sefirot* have historically been portrayed in various configurations, the most important being the Tree of Life.

**Shtetl** (Yiddish) Small town, village.

**Sofer** (pl. **sofrim**) Literally, "scribes." The term refers to the anonymous scribes who explicated Judaism during the approximate era of Persian rule over Palestine.

**Talmud** The summary of the Judaic oral tradition, compiled in writings by sages in Palestine and Babylonia. Completed about 500 C.E., it exists in two editions, one for each center of world Judaism of the time. The Babylonian edition is by far the more comprehensive and authoritative version. The *Talmud* comprises the Mishnah and Gemara.

**Tannaim** Literally, "teachers." The early sages who are mentioned in the Mishnah.

**Tanya** *It Has Been Taught,* the title of the key theoretical work by Rabbi Schneur Zalman of Liady. Its chief section was first published in 1796 and has been intensively studied by Lubavitcher Hasidim and others ever since.

**Teshuvah** "Repentance," or more broadly, return and ascent to one's divine source of origin.

**Tikkun** (pl. **tikkunim**) The divine rectification or redemption of the universe. Every human act, word, and even thought is believed to aid or impede this process.

**Torah** In a narrow sense, the Pentateuch. More generally, Torah is understood to comprise the twenty-four books of the Bible and the Talmud.

**Tohu** Confusion, chaos.

**Yeshiva** (pl. **yeshivot**) House of Study; Hebrew day school.

**Yezer ha-rah** The so-called evil inclination, which motivates human behavior.

**Yezer Tov** The so-called good inclination, which motivates human behavior.

**Zaddik** (pl. **zaddikim**) "Righteous One." In Hasidism, the *zaddik* is the spiritual leader of the community and is viewed as an intermediary between it and the divine world.

**Zohar** The *Book of Splendor,* which first appeared in late thirteenth-century Spain. It is the bible of the Kabbalah and its most influential work. Ascribed to Simon bar Yochai of the second century by traditionalists, scholars today attribute it to Moses de Leon, who is said to have composed most of it in the 1280s and 1290s.

# BIBLIOGRAPHY

Abulafia, Abraham ben Samuel. *The Path of the Names*. Translated and adapted by Bruria Finkel, Jack Hirschman, David Meltzer, and Gershom Scholem. Berkeley: Trigram, 1976.

Amsel, Abraham. *Judaism and Psychology*. New York: Feldheim, 1977.

Ausubel, Nathan. *A Treasury of Jewish Folklore*. New York: Crown, 1961.

*The Baal Shem Tov on Pirkey Avoth*. Translated by Charles Wengrov. Jerusalem: Feldheim, 1974.

Bachya, ben Joseph ibn Paquda. *Duties of the Heart, volumes 1 and 2*. Translated by Moses Hyamson. Jerusalem: Feldheim, 1978.

*Bahir*. Translated by Aryeh Kaplan. New York; Weiser, 1980.

Bokser, Ben Zion. *The Legacy of Maimonides*. New York: Philosophical Library, 1950.

*Book of Creation*. Translated by Irving Freidman. New York: Weiser, 1977.

Cohen, Abraham. *Everyman's Talmud*. New York: Dutton, 1949.

Cordovero, Moses. *The Palm Tree of Deborah*. Translated by Louis Jacobs. New York: Sepher-Hermon Press, 1981.

Dov Baer of Lubavitch. *Tract on Ecstasy*. Translated by Louis Jacobs. London: Vallentine Mitchell, 1963.

Eckman, Lester. *The History of the Musar Movement, 1840–1945*. New York: Shengold, 1975.

Ehrmann, Naftali Hertz. *The Rav*. Translated by Karen Paritzky. Jerusalem: Feldheim, 1977.

*Ethics of the Fathers*. Translated by Philip Blackman. New York: Judaica Press, 1964.

Finkelstein, Louis. *Akiba: Scholar, Saint and Martyr*. New York: Atheneum, 1978.

Fleer, Gedaliah. *Rabbi Nachman's Foundation*. New York: Ohr MiBreslov, 1976.

Friendenwald, Harry. *The Jews and Medicine, volume 1*. Baltimore: The Johns Hopkins University Press, 1934.

Ginzberg, Louis. *The Legends of the Jews, volumes 1–5*. Philadelphia: Jewish Publication Society of America, 1964.

Goldberg, Hillel. *Israel Salanter: Text, Structure, Idea.* New York: Ktav, 1982.

Green, Arthur. The Role of Jewish Mysticism in a Contemporary Theology of Judaism. *Shefa Quarterly,* September 1979, *1*(4), 25–40.

*The Haffetz Hayyim on Pirkey Avoth.* Translated by Charles Wengrov. Jerusalem: Feldheim, 1975.

Hill, Dorothy. *Abraham: His Heritage and Ours.* Boston: Beacon, 1957.

Hoffman, Edward. "The Kabbalah: Its Implications for Humanistic Psychology. "Journal of Humanistic Psychology, Winter 1980, *20* (1), 33–47.

Hoffman, Edward. *The Way of Splendor: Jewish Mysticism and Modern Psychology.* Boulder: Shambhala, 1981.

Jacobs, Louis. *Hasidic Prayer.* New York: Schocken, 1978.

———. *Hasidic Thought.* New York: Schocken, 1976.

———. *Jewish Mystical Testimonies.* New York; Schocken, 1978.

Jung, Carl. Foreword. *The I Ching.* The Richard Wilhelm translation, rendered into English by Carry F. Baynes. Princeton University Press, 1967.

Kaplan, Aryeh. *Chasidic Masters.* Brooklyn: Maznaim, 1984.

———. *Meditation and the Bible.* New York: Weiser, 1978.

Katz, Dov. *The Musar Movement.* Tel Aviv, Israel: Orly Press, 1977.

Katz, Steven T. *Jewish Philosophers.* New York: Bloch, 1975.

Klapholtz, Yisroel Yaakov. *Tales of the Baal Shem Tov, volumes 1–3.* Translated by Abigail Nadav and Sheindel Weinbach. Bnei-Brak, Israel: Yisroel Klapholtz, Rechov Belz 3, 1970–1971.

Kushner, Lawrence. *The Book of Letters.* New York: Harper & Row, 1975.

Labovitz, Annette. *Secrets of the Past, Bridges to the Future.* Miami: Central Agency for Jewish Education, 1983.

Luzzatto, Moses Chaim. *The Knowing Heart.* Translated by Shraga Silverstein. Jerusalem: Feldheim, 1982.

———. *The Path of the Just.* Translated by Shraga Silverstein. Jerusalem: Feldheim, 1966.

———. *The Way of God.* Translated by Aryeh Kaplan. Jerusalem: Feldheim, 1978.

Maimonides, Moses. *The Commentary to Mishnah Aboth.* Translated by Arthur David. New York: Bloch, 1968.

———. *The Guide for the Perplexed.* Translated by Moses Friendlander. New York: Dover, 1964.

———. *The Preservation of Youth.* Translated by H. L. Gordon. New York: Philosophical Library, 1958.

Marcus, Rebecca B. *Moses Maimonides.* New York: Franklin Watts, 1969.

Margolis, Max L. and Alexander Marx. *A History of the Jewish People.* New York: Harper & Row, 1967.

Maslow, Abraham. *Toward A Psychology of Being.* New York: Van Nostrand, 1968.

Meltzer, David. *The Secret Garden: An Anthology in the Kabbalah.* New York: Seabury, 1976.

Minkin, Jacob S. *The World of Moses Maimonides.* New York: Thomas Yoseloff, 1957.

Montefiore, C. G. *A Rabbinic Anthology.* Philadelphia: Jewish Publication Society, 1960.

Munk, Michael L. *The Wisdom in the Hebrew Alphabet.* Brooklyn: Mesorah Publications, 1983.

Neugroschel, Joachim. *Yenne Velt: The Great Works of Jewish Fantasy and Occult.* New York: Pocket Books, 1976.

Neusner, Jacob. *Invitation to the Talmud.* New York: Harper & Row, 1984.

———. *Method and Meaning in Ancient Judaism.* Missoula, Montana: Scholars Press, 1979.

Newman, Louis I. *The Hasidic Anthology.* New York: Schocken, 1975.

———. *Maggidim and Hasidim: Their Wisdom.* New York: Bloch, 1962.

———. *Talmudic Anthology.* New York: Behrman House, 1945.

*Oxford Annotated Bible.* Edited by Herbert G. May and Bruce M. Metzger. New York: Oxford University Press, 1962.

Pliskin, Zelig. *Gateway to Happiness.* Monsey, New York: The Jewish Learning Exchange, 1983.

*Rabbi Nachman's Advice.* Translated by Avraham Greenbaum. Brooklyn: Breslov Research Institute, 1983.

*Rabbi Nachman's Stories.* Translated by Aryeh Kaplan. Brooklyn: Breslov Research Institute, 1983.

*Rabbi Nachman's Wisdom.* Translated by Areyh Kaplan. Brooklyn: Aryeh Kaplan, 1976.

Raphael, Chaim. *The Walls of Jerusalem.* New York: Knopf, 1968.

Rappoport, Angelo S. *Myth and Legend of Ancient Israel.* New York: Ktav, 1966.

———. *A Treasury of the Midrash.* New York: Ktav, 1968.

Rosenblatt, Samuel. *The High Ways to Perfection of Abraham Maimonides.* New York: Feldheim, 1970.

Rosenthal, Gilbert S. *Four Paths to One God.* New York: Bloch, 1973.

———. *Maimonides: His Wisdom for Our Time.* New York: Funk and Wagnalls, 1969.

Rosner, Fred. *The Medical Aphorisms of Maimonides, volume 1.* New York: Bloch, 1973.

Sachar, Abraham. *A History of the Jews.* New York: Knopf, 1972.

Schacter, Zalman M. *Fragments of a Future Scroll.* Germantown, Pennsylvania: Leaves of Grass Press, 1975.

Schacter, Zalman M. and Edward Hoffman. *Sparks of Light: Counseling in the Hasidic Tradition.* Boulder: Shambhala, 1983.

Sandmel, Samuel. *Judaism and Christian Beginnings.* New York: Oxford University Press, 1978.

Schatz, Morris. *Ethics of the Fathers in the Light of Jewish History.* New York: Bloch, 1970.

Schneur Zalman of Liady. *Tanya.* Translated by N. Mindel. Brooklyn: Kehot Publication Society, 1973.

Scholem, Gershom. *Major Trends in Jewish Mysticism.* New York: Schocken, 1974.

Schwartz, Howard. *Elijah's Violin.* New York: Harper & Row, 1983.

———. *Gates to the New City.* New York: Avon, 1983.

Spero, Moshe Halevi. *Judaism. Halakhic Perspectives.* New York: Ktav, 1980.

Silver, Daniel J. *A History of Judaism.* New York: Basic Books, 1974.

Singer, Isaac B. *Reaches of Heaven.* New York: Farrar, Straus & Giroux, 1980.

Steinberg, Milton. *As A Driven Leaf.* New York: Behrman House, 1939.

Steinsaltz, Adin. *The Essential Talmud.* Translated by Chaya Galai. New York: Basic Books, 1976.

Twersky, Isadore. *A Maimonides Reader.* New York: Behrman House, 1972.

Ury, Zalman F. *Studies in Torah Judaism.* New York: Yeshiva University Press, 1970.

Vilnay, Zev. *Legends of Jerusalem.* Philadelphia: Jewish Publication Society of America, 1973.

Weiss, Raymond L. and Charles Butterworth. *Ethical Writings of Maimonides.* New York: Dover, 1983.

Werblowsky, R. J. Zwi. *Joseph Karo, Lawyer and Mystic.* Philadelphia: Jewish Publication Society of America, 1977.

Wiesel, Elie. *Souls on Fire: Portraits and Legends of Hasidic Masters.* New York: Random House, 1972.

Zirin, Edward. *The Birth of the Torah.* New York: Dutton, 1962.

*Zohar,* volumes 1–5. Translated by Harry Sperling and Maurice Simon. London: Soncino Press, 1931-1934.

# INDEX